The
SAGE COTTAGE
Herb Garden Cookbook

The
SAGE COTTAGE
Herb Garden Cookbook

—

Celebrations, Recipes, and Herb Gardening Tips
for Every Month of the Year

by
Dorry Baird Norris

The
Globe
Pequot
press

OLD SAYBROOK, CONNECTICUT

Cover illustration by Margaret Hewitt
Text illustrations by Mauro Magellan

Library of Congress Cataloging-in-Publication Data
Norris, Dorry, Baird.
  The Sage Cottage herb garden cookbook : celebrations, recipes, and herb gardening tips for every month of the year/by Dorry Baird Norris.—1st ed.
      p.   cm.
    ISBN 0-87106-239-9
    1. Cookery (Herbs) 2. Herbs. 3. Herb gardens—New York (State)
  4. Sage Cottage Bed and Breakfast (Trumansburg, N.Y.) I. Title.
  TX819.H4N68   1991
  641.6'57—dc20   91-4193
                                                                      CIP

Book design by Nancy Freeborn
Cover design by Shankweiler Sealy Design
Manufactured in the United States of America
First Edition/Second Printing

Table of Contents

TABLE *of* CONTENTS

TABLE *of* CONTENTS

Acknowledgments

Books, like bouquets, achieve their effect from a variety of textures and fragrances. The fragrance and beauty of this book comes from the contributions of many people.

Twigs of sycamore and lemon signify the curiosity and zest that participants brought to our weekly herb classes at Sage Cottage. There's a bit of rosemary too, for the fond memories they shared with us.

For the last eight years, good friends in the Auraca Herbarists have added mint, orange blossoms, and angelica to my herb life. Their wisdom and generosity of spirit have been an inspiration.

The blue borage and delicate hepatica remind me of the courage and confidence it took for Linda McCandless, editor of *The Grapevine*, to decide that my first, mostly handwritten column had possibilities as a regular feature. Many of these pieces, in somewhat different form, first appeared in the *Vine*.

That delicate sprig of flax is my heartfelt thank-you to the Mesa Public Library in Los Alamos, New Mexico, for the opportunity, over the last five winters, to spend untold hours with their fine collection.

Lupine and holly—imagination and foresight—are a tribute to Betsy Amster at Globe Pequot, who believed that in *Sage Advice* there were the makings of a book.

Laura Strom's sensitive editing of the original manuscript is deserving of great armloads of mimosa, and her patience in the process of making this book work, with handfuls of chamomile.

Copy editor Norma Ledbetter and developmental editors Doe Boyle and Cary Hull contribute ivy for fidelity and white chrysanthemums to our mix. They have, throughout the editing process, remained faithful to my original intent while being ruthless in checking details that will make the book more useful to the reader.

And last, for Roy Thaler, who has tasted all the recipes and read all the words, again and again and again, I offer dock for his patience, southernwood for the constancy of his support, scarlet fuchsia for the comfort he afforded when the project bogged down, and in the center of it all a bright, red tulip.

Introduction

When I first opened the mythical door marked "Herbs" I expected to find little more than a tidy cupboard stocked with hundreds of neatly labeled jars filled with all manner of good things to make my cooking more exciting. Instead, I faced a green corridor lined with doors that stretched beyond the mind's imagining. As I made a beeline toward the door labeled "Cooking," I passed others marked "Cosmetics," "Religion," and "History," beyond which I could see "Myth," "Magic," "Medicine," "Superstition," and "Business."

Flinging open the door labeled "Cooking," I found a vast kitchen. Here was Adrien Petit, Thomas Jefferson's chef, scurrying about looking for tarragon vinegar; over there was Apicius directing an army of Roman cooks, no doubt preparing for an orgy. Through the kitchen window, I could see a well-tended kitchen garden with meadows and orchards and, beyond that, jungles where exotic spices flourished in the sweltering heat. All the food, all the herbs that humankind has seen fit to eat, lay stretched out before me like a giant patchwork quilt.

Once upon a time, country cooking relied on the bounty of the farm and field seasoned with whatever plants tasted good. Recipes called for cream and eggs and butter in astonishing amounts. Today, we lead less active (though more stressful) lives and are told on every hand that many of those wholesome, natural ingredients are harmful.

In ages past, the human race consumed more than 350 plants in the course of a year. Today, that total, in spite of fancy grocery stores, is down to about fifty. Seven years ago, when we first started offering herb classes at Sage Cottage, I resolved to create herb recipes, using the widest possible spectrum of ingredients that were good for people *and* tasted good. We cut out the salt, cut back on sugars, eliminated most of the saturated fats, and cut down on other fats. We offered new tastes and as wide a variety of foods as possible, focusing on complex carbohydrates, fruits, and vegetables. Using the same criteria that the American Dietetic Association has promulgated, each month we offered a different program of our original herb dishes, soliciting comments on the foods from our visitors.

As each program begins, guests are invited to wander through the kitchen garden sniffing and tasting the herbs to be used in the day's menu. At the tasting that follows, their comments about the various dishes are solicited and studied carefully, often resulting in the modification of recipes during the course of the month. This book is a collection of those recipes. It is *not* a diet cookbook, but the food is healthful and, for the most part, easy to make.

At the same time I was creating recipes, I was opening all those other doors in the house of herbs. I explored those rooms and shared stories about herbs and their influence on our lives with the people who joined us each week to taste our Kitchen Garden. From this rich herbal lore, other gardens emerged. The Smiling Island is a medicinal garden, The Beauty Corner shows off herbs that have been used for beauty treatment over the centuries, and the Weaver's Berm contains plants used for dye, fabric, and protecting materials. The Kitchen Garden expanded, and another level was developed for the tea herbs. Beyond that, closer to the barn, is the Bride's Garden, and across the flagstone path the Good Spell Garden overflows with herbs that are supposed to make good things happen. The subtle fragrance of herbs permeates the air. The variety of textures and greens soothes the spirit. The central purpose of all the gardens at Sage Cottage is to help everyone get to know the herbs, the people, and the places that have played such a vital role in who we were, who we are, and who we will become.

Whether your garden is a window box, a manicured parterre, or an untidy jumble of herbs (like mine), use what you grow. Experiment. Introduce your family to new tastes and a more healthful diet. Create your own herb recipes. Explore. Find your own way along the Great Green Hallway that leads back to that first Garden.

A PRIMER ON COOKING WITH HERBS

If herb cooking is a whole new vocabulary for you, then start by tasting the herbs on your shelf. Learn all you can about the fun and flavor available in your garden. You'll discover zesty alternatives to the salt, sugar, and fat that plague our modern diet.

Since time immemorial, *Homo sapiens* has used the bounty of plants to make food taste better as well as to make medicine and to cast spells. For pennies you can fill your cupboard with a wealth of flavors and make yourself privy to the myths and mystery that surround these ancient plants. Bought in tiny tins or fancy glass bottles, herbs and spices can be pricey, but bulk buying in small amounts is a bargain. You'll save money, and you'll also be assured of a cupboard full of fresh herbs.

Parsley, Sage, Rosemary, and Thyme

If you don't have a garden, head to your nearest health-food or bulk-food outlet with this list in hand. For starters, you'll need anise seed, basil, bay leaf, caraway, chili powder, and cinnamon. Measure out some coriander seed and some dill weed, some ground mace, and a scoop of marjoram. Add peppercorns, rosemary, sage, savory, tarragon, and thyme to your collection. You'll need less than an ounce of each. Check the weights (an ounce of dill weed takes up a lot more space than an ounce of chili powder). Be sure to label the bags carefully so that you know what you have.

From the produce section, collect a piece of ginger root, a clove of garlic, and a big bunch of parsley (the flat-leaved kind if you can find it) and head for home. At home, take a few moments to taste your goodies. Rub a pinch of each between your fingers to release the essential oils; put a bit on the tip of your tongue, and let it seep back in your mouth; then swallow. The taste buds in the various parts of your mouth sense different tastes. Sampling herbs, like tasting wine, gives you a variety of sensations. You have 10,000 taste buds in your mouth—give them a chance to work. Think about each taste and file it away so that you know what flavors you have in your cupboard.

There's sweet, piney rosemary for remembrance and fragrant thyme for courage. Sharp tarragon ("tis highly cordial and friendly to the head, heart, and liver"), soothing dill, and sage ("that maketh the lamp of life, so long as nature lets it burn, burn brightly") will fill your kitchen with glorious fragrances.

To retain all those wonderful tastes, keep your dried herbs in small glass containers with tight-fitting lids. Herbs deteriorate quickly when exposed to air, light, and heat. Above the stove is *not* the place to store herbs. Your garlic belongs in a ceramic jar tucked away in a cool, dry place. Stored in the refrigerator, it may start to sprout and will taste bitter. Wrap fresh ginger tightly in plastic wrap and keep in the freezer. To use, slice or grate the amount needed from the frozen root.

Using herbs is easy as long as you taste as you cook. Don't become a slave to a recipe. If you decide when you're tasting the herbs that rosemary isn't your bag, use less than the recipe calls for. When just beginning to cook with herbs, add about three-quarters of the amount called for in the recipe; then taste and add the remainder if you think it would improve the taste. It's easy to add more but impossible to take seasonings out of your cooking. We've come a long way since herbs and spices were used to cover the taste of spoiled food. Remember that herbs are used to enhance the flavor of food, not mask it.

Storage

Arrange your herbs alphabetically on a cool, dry shelf in a covered container marked with the purchase date.

How Much to Use

- The general rule is to use 1 teaspoon of dried herbs for each two servings.
- Use three times as much of the fresh herb as the dry. Then taste! Taste! Taste!

For Best Flavor

- Soak dry herbs in the recipe liquid before adding to the dry ingredients.
- When combining herbs with steaming liquids, measure them away from the stove; then rub them between your palms to release the volatile oils as you drop them into the liquid.

- Herbs produce the best flavor when half of them are added to soups and stews for the last fifteen minutes of cooking. Garlic and bay are exceptions and should be in the pot from the beginning.

- Allow salad dressings to sit for ten or fifteen minutes before tossing with the greens. For an entirely new taste, toss greens with oil and vinegar, crumble herbs over top, and then toss again.

- To make dried herbs taste fresh, sprinkle over a sprig of parsley, mince together, and add to recipe as directed.

- As mentioned in another chapter, there is little point in buying dried parsley. The fresh is available year-round at moderate cost and is infinitely more satisfactory for cooking, just as fresh garlic is superior to garlic powder. Snip the tips off the stems of the parsley, submerge them in a half inch of water in a glass, cover with a plastic bag, and store in the refrigerator (see page 91 for more information on storing fresh herbs). Change the water every few days.

———

Collecting and Drying Herbs

Harvesting

- Pick just as the flower buds are about to open.
- Choose a sunny day after the dew has dried.
- Gather perennials by cutting back one third except cut mints, sweet marjoram, chives, and oregano to 1 inch above the ground.
- Cut parsley, chervil, lovage, and caraway leaves to the ground at the edges of the plant, leaving the crown intact. Cut dill weed and fennel stalks back to the main stem
- Collect in small amounts and handle carefully.

Drying

To dry successfully, herbs need shade, good air circulation, and warmth (75° to 100° F).

- For small-leaved plants, hang in small bunches, away from walls.
- For more moist, larger-leaved plants (basil, lovage, etc.), remove leaves from stem and spread on frames or screens.
- To dry in the *oven:* Spread herbs on a cookie sheet or brown paper bag, turn oven to 100° F and leave oven door open. Turn and check leaves frequently. Drying will take up to an hour, depending on the weather.
- To dry in the *microwave:* Place a single layer of stems or leaves on a paper towel and cover with another paper towel. Zap on high for 1 minute. Check; continue processing at 1-minute intervals until leaves are dry but not crisp.

DECEMBER

Hemlock and cedar,
rosemary, thyme and basil,
frankincense and myrrh,
mistletoe, fir and
the sweet spices of the east.

The plants that we cherish for our winter celebrations are, as William Hamilton said in another context, "the spokes sticking out from the wheel of ancient civilization." As the earth lies dead and cold, the rich scents of the holiday herbs remind us of growing things, of sunshine and gentle rains. The evergreens, fragrant and bright, speak of life everlasting. Close your eyes and breathe in the scent of sweet greens and the rich spices of the Orient.

The lore that surrounds midwinter greenery reaches back through the dark corridors of uncertain times when, as days shortened, our ancestors were terrified lest their world be overwhelmed by cold and darkness. As the days raced toward the winter solstice—that day of the longest night—fires were lit and living greens were gathered in tribute to those spirits who controlled the seasons. It is with this long night, a time of rest in the garden, that our year truly begins.

We all are but a tiny part of the ever-moving stream of the seasons and the years that slip by without our notice. Sit back and think of the generations who have greeted the winter solstice with the same scent filling their nostrils. Reflect . . . celebrate!

SAINT NICHOLAS'S DAY
December 6

Ginger

In the United States, we think of Saint Nicholas as arriving on Christmas Eve, December 24. But in Holland "Sinterklaas," a commanding presence in his bishop's garb, tucks gifts of fruit and candy into the straw-filled wooden shoes of eager Dutch children on the eve of his feast day, December 6.

Because we're all trying to cut back on sweets these days, the sugar plums Clement Moore evoked for Christmas Eve dreams in "The Night Before Christmas" are in short supply at Sage Cottage. But there are always thin, crisp ginger cookies for a guilt-free nibble. Ginger, cinnamon, cardamom, cloves—their scent fills the house with warm memories of love and of Christmases past.

Ginger
Zingiber officinale

The warmest of these spices is ginger. As John Gerard wrote in *The Herbal* (1557), "It is right good with meate in sauces . . . for it is of a heat-

2

ing and digesting qualitie." One of the first spices to reach Europe from Asia, ginger (*Zingiber officinale*) is still one of the most widely used spices throughout the world. By the fourteenth century, the English use of it rivaled their use of precious pepper. Later, the handlike roots found their way to the West Indies, where they flourished.

In European cooking, ginger is most often used in puddings, cakes, and cookies; in India, we find it in everything *but* desserts; the Chinese, revering it as the favorite son of the kitchen god, use it in everything from soup to dessert. Ginger is an important ingredient in salt-free cooking, adding bite and rounding out flavor. Vital to curries and chutneys, a thin slice also punches up the flavor of peach jam and is an invaluable addition to stir-fried dishes.

Ginger soothes the digestive system and is often prescribed for queasy stomachs. A piece of candied ginger will settle your stomach after too much Christmas dinner, as will a cup of ginger tea.

You can buy ginger in many forms: fresh from the produce counter, powdered in the spice section, candied, or preserved in syrup. The knobby, brown fresh root is the most flavorful form; the stems and tiny new knobs have a more gentle taste.

Mace and nutmeg both come from the seed of the apricotlike fruit of *Myristica fragrans*, an evergreen indigenous to the East Indies. The seed itself we use as nutmeg; the lacy scarlet cage (aril) is stripped off and dried as mace. Of the two, mace is a bit more pungent but, to my taste, cleaner and sweeter. It enhances the taste of lemon desserts, improves French toast, pound cake, and oyster stew, and is nice with cherries. Because of its oily base, mace can quickly become rancid, so it must be tightly stoppered and not stored for long periods of time.

Ginger Cutouts

8 DOZEN

These mild but tantalizingly tasty cookies are great for the whole family to make together. They're easy to roll thin and are best that way. A bonus for young cookie bakers: The dough survives considerable rerolling without producing tough cookies. Keep an eye on them in the oven so that they don't get too brown.

Some years at Sage Cottage our cookies are elegantly decorated. Other times, overwhelmed by other tasks, we savor their crunchy zestiness uniced.

1 cup margarine, softened
$1/2$ cup packed brown sugar
$1/3$ cup maple syrup
$1/3$ cup honey
1 teaspoon grated lemon rind
1 teaspoon vanilla extract
$1/2$ teaspoon baking soda
3 tablespoons grated frozen or fresh ginger, loosely placed in
      spoon (or 1 teaspoon ground ginger)
1 teaspoon ground cinnamon
$4^{1}/_{2}$ cups flour ($2^{1}/_{2}$ cups white and 2 cups whole wheat)

Cream margarine and sugar until light; add syrup, honey, lemon rind, vanilla, and soda; beat thoroughly. Add spices and then enough flour to make a soft dough. Press dough into a $1/2$-inch layer on wax paper; cover and chill several hours or overnight.

Divide dough into quarters and use one quarter at a time. Return the remaining dough to refrigerator to keep cold and rollable. On floured board or pastry cloth, using a cloth-covered or well-floured rolling pin, roll dough to $\frac{1}{8}$-inch thickness. Cut in shapes to please your fancy. Place cutouts, not touching, on lightly greased cookie sheet; bake at 350° F for 8 minutes and then check; cookies should be light brown. Bake an additional 2 or 3 minutes if necessary. Repeat with other sections of dough. Press all the scraps together; rechill and cut more cookies.

————

Carrot (Instead-of-Fruit) Cake

SERVES 10–12

If leaden combinations of sugary preserved fruits that sometimes pass for fruitcake aren't your idea of a holiday treat, try this eggless cake instead.

$1\frac{1}{2}$ teaspoons baking soda
$\frac{1}{4}$ cup warm apple juice
$1\frac{1}{2}$ cups grated carrots
$\frac{2}{3}$ cup plain, low-fat yogurt
$\frac{2}{3}$ cup corn oil
$\frac{1}{2}$ cup sugar
$2\frac{1}{4}$ teaspoons ground cinnamon
$\frac{1}{2}$ teaspoon ground mace
$\frac{1}{2}$ teaspoon ground allspice
1 teaspoon grated orange rind
1 cup white all-purpose flour

1 cup whole wheat flour

1 cup raisins, dates, or other dried fruits of your choice

Grease and dust with flour three $5\frac{1}{2}$ x $3\frac{1}{2}$ x 2-inch loaf pans.

Mix baking soda with apple juice and set aside. In a large bowl, mix carrots, yogurt, and oil. Mix in sugar, spices, and orange rind. Combine flours and stir in. Add baking soda–apple juice mixture. Add raisins and stir lightly. Spread in prepared pans. Bake 30 minutes at 350° F and check with a cake tester or thin knife. Knife should come out clean. Cool on racks. When cool, wrap in foil to freeze or serve with eggnog, wassail, or cider.

A Ginger Garden

It's fun and easy to grow your own ginger, a great winter project for young or old. In late fall, pick out a plump "hand" with lots of "eyes." Cut off a piece about 2 inches long and place in a 10-inch pot that is three-quarters full of good potting soil. Cover with more soil, water, place in a sunny window, and watch the tiny green spears emerge. Ginger loves warm, humid places and a once-a-month feeding with dilute fish emulsion. When the stems die down, you can dig up the root for use, reserving a bit for next year's crop, or you can plant it out in the garden when the weather warms.

SAINT LUCY'S DAY
December 13

Saffron and Cardamom

In Sweden, at dawn on Saint Lucy's Day, the youngest daughter of the household, wearing a crown of bilberries (*Vaccinium myrtillus*) alight with candles, wakes her family with coffee and pastries as bright as her crown. A visit to the barn, with goodies for the farmhands and extra rations to the farm animals, is followed by a trip to church. There, homage is paid to Saint Lucy, who brought sight to the blind and food to the hungry. Like her, the *Lucibrud* (Lucy Bride) wearing her glowing crown brings light to the congregation, reminding them of the summer to come, of green growing things, and of plentiful food for all. Golden saffron, a plant of the sun, seems to reflect the glow of the candles in the Lucibrud's crown and is the traditional flavoring for breakfast treats on Saint Lucy's Day.

Saffron
Crocus sativus

The Magi brought the Christ child gold, frankincense, and myrrh but could as easily have shown their adoration with precious saffron (*Cro-*

cus sativus), still the world's costliest spice. Collecting the three precious red stigmas from each fall-blooming flower is delicate work; it takes 4,000 flowers to produce an ounce of this bitterly aromatic herb with its faint taste of iodine.

The saffron flower is depicted on Bronze Age pottery jugs found in Crete and was listed as a medicine in the Papyrus Ebers that may date as far back as 2650 B.C. The seafaring Vikings ranged all the way to Constantinople on their voyages, so saffron and other precious spices, such as cardamom, probably arrived in Scandinavia by the end of the ninth century. The first saffron corms appeared in England during the reign of Edward III (fourteenth century). It soon became an important crop, for, unlike most of the other precious spices, *Crocus sativus* survives the cold. In *The Forme of Cury*, the first cookbook written in English, a large portion of the recipes call for the costly red threads. Saffron is also frequently used in East Indian, Mexican, and Spanish cooking for flavoring rice, bouillabaisse, and curries.

Cardamom (*Elettaria cardamomum*), the second or third most valuable spice, is a member of the ginger family. The brown or tan papery pod contains ten or more spicy black seeds. The northern passion for cardamom is completely eclipsed by the Arab countries' use of this powerfully aromatic and spicy seed. Welcome in baked goods and in curry, the seeds are also used as a breath freshener, in coffee, and in ground-meat dishes. Apples welcome a dash of ground cardamom ($1/2$ teaspoon per 4 cups of prepared apples) as do sweet winter vegetables like turnip, rutabaga, and winter squash. Swedes enjoy the warm taste of cardamom throughout the year, but at no time is it more appreciated than when scenting a crusty royal crown of sweet bread on Saint Lucy's Day.

Saint Lucy's Golden Cats

APPROXIMATELY 10 CATS

Golden saffron buns delight the palate. The buns are baked in the form of cats, for it was said that Saint Lucy was able to rout the devil, who often appeared in homes in the form of a cat. Serve with generous bowls of lemon-laced hot applesauce, mugs of coffee to which you've added a crushed seed or two of cardamom, and cinnamon-laced cocoa for the kids.

¼ teaspoon saffron
2 tablespoons boiling water
1 teaspoon maple syrup
1 recipe Sour Milk Herb Biscuits (page 206) made with half
    white and half whole wheat flour
a few currants for eyes

Combine saffron, boiling water, and maple syrup; put aside to cool.

Following directions for Sour Milk Herb Biscuits, roll out as directed. Using small cat cookie cutter, cut dough in biscuits. Place biscuits ½ inch apart on a cookie sheet. Use a pastry brush to thoroughly coat the top and sides of the biscuits with the saffron mixture; add currants for eyes. Bake in a 425° F oven for 10 to 12 minutes or until biscuits are golden brown.

Cardamom Prune Crown

3 LOAVES OR 1 LARGE "CROWN"

$3/4$ pound soft pitted prunes
2 packages dry yeast
2 tablespoons orange juice concentrate
1 cup lukewarm water
$2\frac{1}{2}$ cups white all-purpose flour
$2\frac{1}{2}$ cups whole wheat all-purpose flour
$1/4$ cup dry milk powder
1 teaspoon crushed cardamom seed
$1/2$ cup warm water
1 teaspoon grated lemon peel
2 egg whites, lightly beaten

If prunes are soft, chop. If they are dry, cover with boiling water, allow to stand until cool, drain, and then chop.

Add orange juice concentrate to lukewarm water, sprinkle yeast over the top. Allow to stand until yeast is dissolved and foamy.

In a large bowl, combine 2 cups white and 2 cups whole wheat flour, cardamom, and dry milk powder. Add yeast mixture, $1/2$ cup water, lemon peel, and egg whites to the dry ingredients, stirring very well. Cover with plastic wrap and let rise in a warm place until doubled in bulk. Stir in chopped prunes.

Pour the remaining flours on a board and turn the dough out onto the flour. Knead until all the flour is absorbed and the dough is elastic. Spray or lightly grease three $3\frac{1}{4}$ x $7\frac{1}{4}$-inch loaf pans or one large bundt pan with vegetable shortening and sprinkle lightly with flour. For three loaves, divide batter into thirds, roll out, and then shape into three loaves. For crown, roll dough into a 24x4-inch rectangle, rolling the dough up from the long edge. Starting with the outside edge of the pan and working inward, coil the dough around the center post. Press down lightly. Cover pans with a damp cloth and allow to rise until doubled in bulk. Bake small loaves in a preheated 365° F oven (it must be slightly lower than 375° F) for 35 minutes. Bake the larger pan for 45 to 50 minutes. Check after 30 minutes; if top is browning too quickly, cover lightly with foil.

Gold in the Garden

Saffron's thin, spearlike leaves appear in the spring and then die down. The purple, lilylike blossoms emerge in the fall after much of the herb garden has collapsed.

When purchasing corms, make sure you get *Crocus sativus*. Be careful not to confuse it with the autumn crocus (*Colchicum autumnale*), a powerful drug.

Crocuses like well-drained, loose soil with a bit of grit added. The corms can be planted 4 to 6 inches deep in August (they will bloom in upstate New York in October). They want well-drained, rich but gritty soil and need to be dug up every three or four years and divided. Be sure to mark the spot well so that you don't plant over them in your spring enthusiasm for filling in the garden. Mine seem to survive nicely with only a half day's sun.

THE BOSTON TEA PARTY
December 16

Herb Teas

No engraved invitations were sent out for the Boston Tea Party. Blankets and feathers rather than white gloves and straw bonnets were the order of the day when those hardy New Englanders gathered at Griffen's wharf that fateful December day in 1773 to protest the unfair tax on imports. On December 16, let's pay homage to those men and ladies, who, throughout the long fight for independence, went assiduously about the task of discovering substitutes for unfairly taxed imported tea. The women had pledged: "We the daughters of those patriots who do now appear for the public interest, . . . do with pleasure engage with them in denying ourselves the drinking of foreign TEA in hopes to frustrate a plan which tends to deprive a whole community of what is most valuable in life."

For them, tea made from the local flora was the brew of patriots. Astringent raspberry (*Rubus canadensis*) and blackberry (*Rubus occidentalis*) leaves, the red-rooted New Jersey

Anise hyssop
Agastache foeniculum

tea (*Ceanothus americanus*), goldenrod (*Soldago odora*), spice bush (*Lindera benzoin*), and Oswego tea (*Monarda didyma*) all made an appearance in the teapots of the revolutionaries.

Since very ancient times, beverages from the leaves, bark, roots, and stems of plants have been used both for pleasure and as medicine. A resurgence of interest in tea from botanicals grew out of the natural-food movement of the 1960s. Now, the grocery shelves are packed with all manner of alternative teas.

Are you feeling pressured? Are the short, dark days and too much Christmas hubbub getting you down? Then it's time for a cup of mint tea, with spearmint, *Mentha spicata* having the most pleasant flavor. Mint tea is what we offer nervous bridegrooms at Sage Cottage who have prewedding jitters. Chamomile (*Matricaria recutita*, or *Chamaemelum nobile*) is soothing, too, as long as you're not a hay fever sufferer. Take a sniff of the blossoms when you open the jar, and if you don't get the "sneezles and wheezles," it should be safe for you.

Caution: Moderation is the key to enjoying herb teas without side effects. Remember, even though these are natural products, many of them, in concentrated form, have been used as powerful medicines. Sweet clover, comfrey, nutmeg, ginseng, kava, and St. John's wort can cause problems. Parsley tea should be avoided by pregnant women, and many experts advise that children not be given any herb teas.

The tender, scented geraniums (*Pelargonium* var.)—rose, peppermint, and lemon—winter gratefully in the house and, with a dash of honey, make a sweet tea while also benefiting from a bit of pruning.

Seeds from the store, caraway (*Carum carvi*), licoricelike fennel (*Foeniculum vulgare*), star anise (*Illicium verum*), and maple-flavored fenugreek (*Trigonella foenum graecum*), as well as the old reliables coriander (*Coriandrum sativum*) and dill (*Anethum graveolens*), are good in the teapot, too. The brews made from seeds seem more filling than the leaf teas. (Make a New Year's resolution to enjoy them also in January when you are trying to drop a few of those unwelcome holiday pounds.)

Lift your steaming cup in a toast to the women of the Revolution who, with heart and soul and teacup, joined the fight for independence.

Making Tea

For the perfect cup of tea, use freshly drawn water and heat just to boiling (too much boiling and the water gets flat). Pour some of the boiling water into your ceramic or enamel pot (or cup) to warm it. Empty out the hot water and add 1 teaspoon dried herbs (or 2 teaspoons fresh) for each cup of tea. Then add 1 spoonful for the pot and pour boiling water over all, cover the pot or cup, and allow to steep for 5 minutes. Herb teas don't brew up as dark as regular teas do, so give it a taste test. If you find the tea is too weak, add more herbs, but don't increase the steeping time, as that tends to give an unpleasant, grassy taste to the brew. Fresh herbs, right from the garden, make a delightful beverage. With them, you can often finish your pot of tea and then add one-third the water you did in the first steeping and come up with a respectable second cup or pot.

Herb Tea Blends from Dried Herbs

The real joy of teas from your garden (or the bulk bins) is experimenting to create your own favorite tastes. Rose hips or hibiscus flowers add a tart taste (and a bit of Vitamin C) to sweet herbs. Cloves, cinnamon sticks, or allspice berries add zing and a hint of sweetness to herb teas. Orange or lemon slices (or dried grated rind) both sweeten the tea and tease the palate.

Two M Tea Combine 1 part marjoram leaves, 2 parts mint, and 1 part hibiscus flowers.

Thyme-Mint Tea This is a rich, warm tea. On Sundays after church, ask friends to stop by for spears of toasted Hummingbird Bread (page 151) spread with yogurt cheese and a dollop of white grape jam, all washed down with a cup of Thyme-Mint Tea. You'll probably have to dry your own lemon thyme or use $1/4$ part grated, dried lemon peel. Combine 1 part peppermint, 1 part thyme, 1 part lemon thyme, and $1/4$ part crushed coriander seeds.

A Quick Cuppa Cheer Best made by the cup. Use 1 teaspoon spearmint and a $1/4$-inch slice of fresh ginger, mashed. This tea, served with Barley Sticks (page 267) warms and satisfies on a blustery afternoon.

Iced Teas from Fresh Herbs

Iced herb teas are refreshing and low cal. In the South and Southwest, iced tea is served year round, and herbal iced tea makes a fine, thirst-quenching substitute for soft drinks whatever the season or region. At Sage Cottage, a big, frosty pitcher of cold tea and a full bucket of ice always awaits our guests during the summer. We make a strong infusion, strain, add an equal quantity of cool water, and serve in tall glasses over lots of ice. Ahhhh!

Melissa and Sage Guaranteed to drive away melancholy and make you wise. Lemon Balm (*Melissa officinalis*) loses its flavor when dried, so the best way to enjoy its taste is in the summer. Pineapple sage (*Salvia elegans*) lives up to its name and lends a strong pineapple taste to this mix. Anise hyssop (*Agastache foeniculum*) blends and sweetens the other herbs.

Collect eight 12-inch pieces of lemon balm, four 4-inch pieces of pineapple sage, one 8-inch sprig of anise hyssop and rinse. Bend stems in half, then half again, crushing lightly. Add 5 cups boiling water; steep. Strain into large jar, add 5 cups cold water, and chill. Serve over lots of ice.

Marvelous Mints Just as the best cider comes from a blend of apples, this tea has the richest flavor when concocted with a variety of mints. Any collection will do, but be sure to include at least one stem of mountain mint (*Pycnanthemum pilosum, P. tenufolium*). Collect and rinse ten 12-inch cuttings of mixed mints and proceed as above. Serve garnished with Johnny-jump-ups or anise hyssop flowers.

A Tea Garden
at
Your Back Door

Start planning your own tea garden now. Expand your horizons. Stately anise hyssop (*Agastache foeniculum*), which produces spires of purple flowers nearly all summer, surely deserves a spot toward the back of the garden. At Sage Cottage, the hummingbirds take a taste of these blossoms on their way to gorge themselves on the scarlet bee balm. The strongly flavored mountain mints, both narrow and broad leaved (*Pycnanthemum tenufolium, P. pilosum*), are wonderful dried or fresh and make a grand iced tea. Lemon grass (*Cymbopogon citratus*) needs to winter in the house, but that only adds to its charm, as it's available all year long. It won't mind at all being planted out in the garden during the summer.

Add a few plants each year so that when the cold winds of winter whistle around the house, you can be warm and cozy inside sipping a steaming cup of summer.

WASSAILING
December 31

Allspice and Cinnamon

Wassail! Wassail! over the town,
Our toast is white, our ale it is brown:
Our bowl it is made of the Maplin tree,
We be good fellows all; I drink to thee.

Cinnamon
Cinnamomum

Webster defines *wassail* as an "early English toast to someone's health" or "to sing carols from house to house at Christmas" or "a hot drink made with wine, beer, or cider, spices, sugar, and usually baked apples that is traditionally served in a large bowl especially at Christmas time." The word *wassail* comes from the Middle English *waes haeil*, meaning "be thou well." Carrying the wassail bowl, afloat with apples, Medieval English carolers made their rounds on Christmas or New Year's Eve, visiting the grand houses in the town and singing for coins, Christmas loaf, or a bit of beer.

Apples are the fruit of winter and of Christmas. Wreaths of tiny, decorative lady apples decorated Colonial Williamsburg doors, and apple "trees" are a staple of Christmas decorations in Scandinavia, so cider seems a natural quaff for the season. Roasted apples were an indispensable adornment in the wassailing bowl, and it was customary for each reveler to eat one and wish the assembled crowd good luck. To assure a good crop of apples the following season, the farmer and his family adjourned to the orchard following Christmas supper or on New Year's Eve carrying the wassail. After a toast to the trees, in a celebration that may hark back to pagan sacrifices for Pomona, Roman goddess for fruits and orchards, the remaining drink was poured over the branches of the best-bearing trees in the orchard. This ancient custom of wassailing the trees is a reminder that our traditional winter holiday was in ancient times observed as the Saturnalia, a time to worship the sun. The Romans' solstice ceremony on the "turning of the year," running from December 17 to 23, honored Saturn, god of agriculture, and was directed toward increasing the fertility of nature.

The traditional combination of eggs, sugar, and ale doesn't please this twentieth-century palate, so we offer these lighter and smoother brews, sparkling with sweet herbs and spices, that are especially suited to toasting friends and trees this holiday.

Two of the holiday drinks we serve at Sage Cottage are seasoned with allspice (*Pimenta dioca*), the only spice commercially grown only in the Western Hemisphere. Jamaica produces most of the world's supply of this unripe, dried fruit. Efforts to naturalize it in other parts of the world have failed. It should be noted that *Pimenta dioca* is no relation to the Carolina allspice (*Calcanthus floridas*). Particularly suited to seasoning many of our native crops, allspice wasn't in use in Europe until the seventeenth century, which makes allspice's history the shortest of any of the spices.

Buy whole berries and crush them just before use for the best flavor. You'll find allspice in commercial pickling spices, and it is used to advantage in sauerbraten, in tomato-based sauces (especially catsup and chili sauce), in mincemeat, and discreetly in desserts. A scant ⅛ teaspoonful added to fruit pies along with the other spices or a teeny pinch in pea soup will add surprising punch.

WASSAIL BOWLS

Both the Spicy Wassail and the New England Wassail can be made more authentic by floating baked crab or lady apples in the bowl. If you're in a hurry, pineapple chunks heated in the brew can be used instead.

Serve these drinks to icy-fingered carolers or to welcome in the New Year, and may your trees and your friendships both bear fruit beyond measure. Five Roses Eggless Applesauce Cake (page 243) and gingersnaps or Ginger Cutouts (page 4) topped with paper-thin slices of low-fat Swiss cheese are delicious accompaniments.

———

Roasted Apples for Wassail Bowls

12 APPLES

Core one dozen crab apples or very small apples. Place in a low pan and sprinkle with 2 tablespoons sugar. Add 2 tablespoons water to the bottom of the pan. Bake at 375° F for $\frac{1}{2}$ hour or until apples are soft but not mushy. Float hot apples on the wassail.

Spicy Wassail Bowl

TWENTY-FIVE 6-OUNCE SERVINGS

This is a favorite of everyone who samples it. Find an inexpensive basket that your Crockpot will fit into, cut a hole for the cord, and you have the perfect server. For a more Christmasy drink, replace the cider with cranberry juice.

> 1 gallon apple cider
> 1/3 cup dark brown sugar
> 1 12-ounce can undiluted frozen orange juice concentrate
> 1 12-ounce can undiluted frozen lemonade concentrate
> 1 tablespoon whole cloves
> 1 tablespoon allspice berries
> 4 cinnamon sticks (Never substitute ground cinnamon for
>   cinnamon sticks in drinks because it does not blend in.)
> 1 teaspoon ground mace
> 1 teaspoon ground nutmeg

Combine cider, brown sugar, orange juice, and lemonade in a large pan. Tie cloves, allspice, cinnamon, mace, and nutmeg in cheesecloth or muslin and add to cider. Cover and simmer for 15 or 20 minutes. Remove spice bag and serve hot in mugs.

New England Wassail

TWENTY-ONE 6-OUNCE SERVINGS

1 gallon cider
½ cup dark brown sugar
1 tablespoon freshly grated ginger
1 tablespoon allspice berries
1 tablespoon whole cloves
4 cinnamon sticks
½ teaspoon ground nutmeg
2 cups dark rum
2 lemons, cut in thin slices and halved

Place cider and sugar in a large kettle or a crockpot. Tie the ginger, allspice, cloves, cinnamon, and nutmeg in muslin or cheesecloth. Bring to a boil and simmer for 15 minutes. Remove spice bag; add rum and lemon slices. Simmer 10 minutes more. Serve hot.

Glögg

TEN 6-OUNCE SERVINGS

In Scandinavia, glögg, or hot spiced wine, is the winter drink. This one warms the cockles of the coldest heart.

> 4 cups burgundy or medium-dry red wine or purple grape juice
> 4 cups white grape juice
> 1 cup raisins
> 7 whole cardamom pods, crushed slightly
> 8 whole cloves
> 2 cinnamon sticks (do not use ground cinnamon)
> zest from 1 orange, in fine slivers
> 1/2 teaspoon ground ginger

Add wine, grape juice, and raisins to a large pan. Tie spices in muslin or cheesecloth and add to pan. Heat mixture but do not bring to a boil.

Remove spices before serving.

Apple Pomanders

Lady apples or crab apples can be part of your holiday decorations as well as trimmings for the punch bowl if you use them to create tiny (nonedible) pomanders.

Use small, perfect apples and stud each one closely with whole cloves. Mix together $1/4$ cup ground cinnamon, 2 tablespoons ground cloves, 1 tablespoon grated lemon peel, 1 teaspoon ground allspice, 1 teaspoon grated mace, and 2 tablespoons powdered orris root. Roll "cloved" apples in this mixture until they are completely coated. Gently shake off the excess. Spread apples out on a plate or tray and tuck into a large paper bag; seal loosely. Place in a dark, cool place to dry for several weeks. Tie with tiny bows and pile into a glass compote. These can also be hung in closets.

Sometimes the same bugs that attack your flour products settle on pomanders. To prevent this, after the pomanders are thoroughly dry, pop them into the freezer for several hours. Repeat every month or so during the hot weather.

JANUARY

Janus, porter of heaven, was said to have opened its gates each morning to allow the sun out and to have closed them at night to shut it in, thus creating the darkness. The gray-brown days of our Northeastern January often make one wonder whether Janus hasn't deserted his post, leaving the pearly gates just slightly ajar, to head for sunnier climes.

In January, at least for those of us in the Northeast, our gardens are perfect. The seed catalogs come, and we dream the impossible dream of a weed-free garden covered with rich compost, free of bugs and blight, and overflowing with healthful herbs. The dream can become reality if we use this time to plan for the coming year. January is the time to heed Alexander Pope's comment: "My garden, like my life, seems to me every year to want correction and require alteration." The darkest days of winter are past, yet we know that we face stormy days ahead. Good days to pore over seed catalogs, force bulbs, and prepare imaginative food for hearty appetites. Correct and alter your life and your garden to meet the changes.

TWELFTH NIGHT
January 6

Cloves and Other Sweet Spices

Your places lads and lasses take,
to find your fortune in the cake.
The king is he who finds the bean,
yet he may not choose his queen,
The queen is she,
who gets the pea.
Button, button who has it now
to that faithful soul we must bow.
Next let us sing of patience true,
when thimble passes into view.
Ah riches, now hark and take your time,
For it's wealth to thee who finds the dime.
But if ye be smart, ye'll choose the heart,
Love will come to you who finds that part.
The last we seek is clove
in jester's scepter shape.
If that be yours then by jove,
We'll toast thee, fool, with grape.

Clove
Eugenia aromatica

December is always too full, and New Year's Eve parties seem too forced and frantic. This year, welcome the New Year and bid farewell to the Christmas season with a quiet celebration on Twelfth Night, January 6.

The Feast of the Epiphany commemorates the night that the Three Wise Men appeared at the manger in Bethlehem. The legends tell us that Melchior brought gold from Arabia symbolizing the royalty of the new-born child; Caspar, frankincense, symbolic of Christ's divinity; Balthasar, myrrh, an allusion to the sorrows that would be the lot of the Christ child. In the Eastern churches, this day is still celebrated as Christmas.

During the Middle Ages, the Christmas season lasted for twelve days, a relic of the pagan Saturnalian orgies that reached their climax on Twelfth Night. In France, the celebration concluded with the serving of *La Galette du Roi*, a grand cake containing a bean. The lucky one who was served the bean became the King of the Bean and ruled over the evening's raucous games, dancing, and music.

Pickling spice, an emergency spice cupboard in a can, will give the celebration the warming touch that winter gatherings need. Whole peppercorns, cloves, mustard seeds, bay leaves, and chilies are augmented by cardamom, coriander, cinnamon, mace, ginger, and allspice.

The nail-shaped clove (*Eugenia aromatica*), so rough on the fingers when you attempt to punch them into oranges or lemons for pomanders, is the unopened flower of one of the myrtle family. The name derives from the French *clou* or Latin *clavis*, meaning "nail." Oil of cloves has been used to treat toothaches and still scents mouthwashes and toothpastes. Much of the worldwide clove production goes into the production of "kretet" cigarettes (a combination of cloves and tobacco) popular in Indonesia.

Old "receipts" often call for cassia (*Cinnamomum cassia*), a slightly bitter version of the more expensive true cinnamon (*Cinnamomum zeylanicum*). The Food and Drug Administration has chosen to allow both to be sold in this country as "cinnamon." The ancient spices, cited in the Bible as having been used to anoint the temple of the children of Israel, were made from the dried inner bark or shoots of either tree. Regarded by the Chinese as the tree of life, cassia may indeed prolong life, as the antiseptic phenols it contains retard food spoilage. The sweet taste of cinnamon or cassia enhances the flavor of bananas and apples and appears in Middle Eastern meat dishes and Pennsylvania Dutch tomatoes. With bay leaf, it scents Indian rice and curries, and it works wonders on hot cocoa and other chocolate treats.

Your Twelfth Night Cake will choose the royalty for your party and proclaim the fortunes of others. The king will find the bean, the queen the pea, and the jester the clove. The one who discovers the button in his cake is Faithful, and the thimble will single out the Patient one among your guests. The dime will tell of Wealth to come, while the heart speaks of Love. Gather round and toast the season; the new year has begun.

____

Twelfth Night Cake

SERVES 12–16

6 egg whites
$^{1}/_{2}$ cup honey
$^{1}/_{2}$ cup undiluted frozen pineapple juice concentrate
1 tablespoon vegetable oil
1 teaspoon grated lemon rind
$1^{1}/_{2}$ cups plain, low-fat yogurt
1 tablespoon molasses

½ teaspoon vanilla
1½ teaspoons baking powder
1½ teaspoons baking soda
¼ teaspoon ground cardamom
½ teaspoon allspice
1½ teaspoons ground cinnamon
1½ cups whole wheat flour
1½ cups unbleached white flour
½ cup golden raisins
½ cup slivered almonds
¼ cup confectioners' sugar
a dried bean, a dried pea, a clove, a thimble, a button, a dime,
    something heart-shaped, each wrapped separately in
    aluminum foil

Spray a 10-inch bundt pan or a 9x13-inch flat pan with oil and dust lightly with flour. Combine first eight ingredients and beat together. Combine flours, baking powder, soda, and spices; stir lightly into egg-white mixture. Fold in raisins. Pour half of the batter into the cake pan and sprinkle half of the almonds over that batter. Stir remaining almonds into the batter in the bowl. Spread over batter in the pan.

Poke foil-wrapped "fortunes" into the middle of the batter all around the cake, making sure they are far enough apart so that you will be able to cut the cake.

Bake in a 350° F oven for 50 to 60 minutes. Allow to cool for 10 minutes in the pan. Remove from pan and allow to cool on a rack.

When completely cool, sprinkle the top with confectioners' sugar. Serve on your handsomest cake plate and garnish with Christmas herbs.

Pickling-Spice Peach Mold

SERVES 8–10

If you know that your guests are on diets after the holiday and would prefer something lighter than the Twelfth Night Cake, tuck your fortunes into this fruit mold after it starts to jell. Since you can see into this mold, add a few empty foil packets to keep people guessing.

1 2-pound can peach slices packed in light syrup or their own juice
1 cup liquid from peaches
1 tablespoon pickling spice
¼ cup sugar
2 tablespoons gelatin
½ cup cold water
3 cups orange juice
1 tablespoon red wine vinegar
½ teaspoon grated orange rind
1–1½ cups plain, low-fat yogurt

Drain peaches thoroughly, reserving juice. Measure peach juice into small saucepan, adding water, if necessary, to make 1 cup. Add pickling spice and sugar and bring to boil. Lower heat and simmer for 3 minutes. Remove from heat, cover, and steep for 5 minutes. Meanwhile, soak the gelatin in ½ cup cold water in a medium bowl. Strain hot peach juice and spice mixture into gelatin, stirring to dissolve gelatin thoroughly. Stir in orange juice, red-wine vinegar and orange rind. Add peaches to 6-cup fluted mold that has been rinsed with cold water; pour liquid over all. Chill.

When gelatin begins to set, add fortunes. Return to refrigerator and allow the mold to set solidly.

Unmold carefully onto a silver platter and garnish with sprigs of fresh rosemary. Serve with cinnamon-sprinkled yogurt and coffee or tea.

Planning a Perfect Garden

By mid-January, all the new garden catalogs are probably firing your imagination. This is the time to sit down and study the new plants you'd like to add to the garden. Start a file card (4 x 6 inches is a practical size) for each one. Head each card with the botanical and common name of the plant. Copy down what the catalog says about the plant; then go to your other garden books to find out more about your prospective adoptee. What conditions does it like? How hardy is it? What special care does it need? Where will it fit? While you're at it, make up cards on the plants you already have in your garden. Before long, you'll have created a gardening guide tailor-made for *your* garden. Add the source of the seeds or plants that you purchase and the date. This will help to avoid duplication.

During the garden season, make notes on the plants' progress. The following spring, you can check the cards to develop your work plan for next year's growing season.

ROSEMARY DAY
January

The Many Faces of Rosemary

I decree that henceforth and forevermore the dreariest, darkest day in January shall be observed as "Rosemary Day." This is the time to pay homage to this gloriously fragrant plant that we northeasterners haul into the house each fall to nurse through the dark days of winter. At Sage Cottage, I toast the dreary days of January with a steaming cup of fresh rosemary tea.

A native of the Mediterranean, rosemary arrived in Britain with the Roman armies. Its first appearance in the United States was recorded by Captain John Mason in 1606. Writing about New England, John Josselyn noted in his plant list of 1672 that rosemary is "no plant for this country." In upstate New York, rosemaries are treasured and cosseted. Those of us from Zone 5 northward suffer mightily when we hear our gardening friends from the south and west, where rosemary spills over banks and yards, complain of rosemary as a nuisance.

Rosemary
Rosmarinus officinalis

The piney, sweet fragrance filling the air each time the plant is touched is a reminder that rosemary is indeed the herb of remembrance. With the snow falling outside and the wind rattling the windowpanes, the scent recalls sunny hillsides, warm days, and gardens bright with flowers.

Rembert Dodoens, sixteenth-century Dutch physician, wrote in his herbal (later appropriated, in part, by John Gerard) that rosemary "comforteth the braine, the memorie and the inward senses." Centuries before Dodoens, Greek students would twine rosemary in their hair to fortify and refresh the brain at exam time.

Culpeper maintained that "to burn the herb in houses and chambers, correcteth the air in them." Used as a strewing herb in ancient times, it freshened the air of drafty, smoky castles. Tossed on the fire, rosemary flavored many a spit-turned leg of lamb.

Symbol of remembrance and emblem of love, the fragrance of rosemary wafting about the house during the winter or curling about your hand as you brush by it in the summer garden boosts the spirit and according to an old herbal, "will keepe thee youngly."

The dried, needlelike leaves of the rosemary demand light chopping with a sharp knife before being added to dishes. To bite down on a whole needle can be too much of a good thing; some cooks may pass up this sterling herb because they think the flavor is too strong. Chopping also releases the flavor from both the fresh and dried herb. Discreetly used, rosemary is a boon to egg dishes, soup stocks, lamb, and especially chicken.

Rosemary Lamb Stew

SERVES 6

Common practice cautions us not to use two strong herbs together, yet the old musical recipe for "parsley, sage, rosemary, and thyme" is a fine combination, especially when partnered with garlic and lemon in a lamb stew.

2 pounds boneless lamb for stew
1 tablespoon corn oil
2 cloves of garlic, sliced
1 large onion, coarsely chopped
1 cup dry vermouth
6 slices of lemon cut in quarters
4 medium potatoes, cut in quarters
4 medium carrots, cut diagonally in $1/2$-inch slices
1 large onion, coarsely chopped
$1/2$ teaspoon dried rosemary, crumbled (or, even better, 1 teaspoon minced fresh)
$1/2$ teaspoon rubbed dried sage
$1/2$ teaspoon dried thyme
$1/2$ teaspoon freshly ground pepper
$1/4$ cup minced fresh parsley

Heat oil in heavy pan or Dutch oven, add meat, and cook over medium-high heat until brown. Add garlic and 1 onion and cook until translucent. Add vermouth, reduce heat, and scrape the bottom of the pan to loosen all the good brown stuff. Add lemon. Cover and bake in a 325° F oven for 45 minutes.

Add vegetables, including the remaining onion, and cook 30 minutes. Add rosemary, sage, thyme, and pepper and bake an additional 15 or 20 minutes or until vegetables are tender. Serve with toasted French bread, brushed with garlic and olive oil.

———

Baked Rosemary Squash
SERVES 6

This can be made with butternut or acorn squash. The squash is perfumed with a whisper of rosemary and makes a fine accompaniment to the stew. This is also tasty if you replace the rosemary with thyme or lemon thyme.

1$\frac{1}{2}$–2 pound butternut squash or 3 acorn squash
1 tablespoon butter or margarine, melted
6 1-inch sprigs fresh rosemary (or $\frac{1}{2}$ teaspoon dried)
$\frac{1}{4}$ cup cider or apple juice
freshly ground pepper to taste

Cut squash in half; remove seeds. Brush each half with melted butter. Place each butternut squash half, cut-side down, on top of 3 sprigs or $\frac{1}{4}$ teaspoon rosemary in a large pan with sides. (Use 1 sprig or a sprinkle of dried rosemary under each acorn squash half.) Pour in cider; add water to $\frac{1}{4}$ inch. Bake in a 375° F oven for 45 minutes. Turn squash over and bake for an additional 15 minutes or until tender. Scoop squash out of shells, pile lightly in serving dish, and grind fresh pepper over top.

Rosemary Oil

Add four 4-inch sprigs fresh rosemary and 2 cloves garlic to 2 cups virgin olive oil in a 1-pint glass jar. Cover and allow to steep for 10 days to 2 weeks. Strain, squeezing the rosemary to get all the oil out, discard solids, cover, and store oil at room temperature.

• Use to brush on toasted English muffins or French bread. Top with chutney or our Onion Jam (page 81).

• Add 1 teaspoon to 2 cups steamed parsnips; toss and grind a bit of pepper over top.

• Toss 1 pound of cooked new potatoes with 1 teaspoon rosemary oil; shake over heat. Serve topped with minced fresh parsley.

Growing Rosemary Indoors

The big pots of rosemary that grace Sage Cottage's Kitchen Garden, Tea Garden, and Beauty Corner get hosed off in the fall and brought directly into the garden room where they enjoy a filtered southern sun. They prosper in the coolish room. As for the plants that have been growing without pots, I dig deeply around the circumference of their leaf or branch spread, then lift the plant gently from the ground. At this point, it's easy to tell what size pot they'll need. Rosemary likes well-drained soil that's a bit gritty and slightly alkaline. I always work a few eggshells into the sand-perlite mix when I'm potting up rosemaries for the house. Put the plant in the clay pot, firm up the soil around the root ball, and feed with a dilute solution of fish emulsion. Place potted rosemaries on a tray of pebbles; this prevents water from sitting in the pots and provides some added moisture to the area where the plants are growing. Water when the soil is dry, but don't allow the root ball to dry out. Feed very lightly once a month with dilute fish emulsion. If the room heats up during the day, give the plants a quick spritz of warm water.

CHINESE NEW YEAR
January

Daylilies and Stir-Fries

The Chinese New Year falls between the
time the first new moon has left the
sign of Capricorn and entered into
Aquarius (between January 21 and
February 19). It is the most signifi-
cant holiday in the Chinese calendar.
Accounts are settled, houses are
cleaned, and families gather to rejoice
and honor their ancestors. Weeks of
preparation go into the multicourse banquet
served on New Year's Eve.

In the United States, the
Chinese New Year is celebrated
with colorful parades—each featuring a huge silk dragon, the ruler of
rivers, lakes, and seas—that weave
through the streets to the accompaniment of firecrackers and gongs, routing
winter from its hold on the earth.

Chinese culture is the oldest contin-
uous civilization on the globe. By the first century A.D., the Chinese had

Daylily
Hemerocallis flava

incorporated at least 365 plants into their cooking. Their strict class system seems to have encouraged the development of an exquisite cuisine for the rich. The poor, on the other hand, made do with skimpy resources of both food and fuel, eating everything at hand, cut into small pieces to speed cooking and thus preserve precious fuel—a meager but healthful diet. In the manner of the ancients, the Chinese continue to use an astonishing array of plants and fungi for both food and seasoning. Chinese cooking is endlessly interesting, yet can be fast and easy, with wonderful and unique results.

Over the last twenty-five years, we have seen an expansion of Chinese vegetable sections in our grocery stores. Bok choy, fresh ginger, and mung bean sprouts have become commonplace. Rice vinegar and an array of soy and plum sauces crowd the shelves that used to hold only water chestnuts, bamboo shoots, and chow-mein noodles.

Two problems have marred this rosy picture. The use of monosodium glutamate, once a staple in Chinese cooking, causes allergic reactions in some people. Sodium-rich soy sauce, another cornerstone of Chinese cooking, puts many Chinese dishes on the forbidden lists of those on low-salt diets. The manufacturers have responded by creating so-called "low-salt" soy sauces. These sauces are still loaded with sodium, 110 milligrams per $\frac{1}{2}$ teaspoon, but if you dilute the soy sauce with red wine (one part soy sauce to two parts wine), you produce a great tasting and more healthful alternative.

The yin and yang of sweet and sour are a boon to those looking for interesting foods without a lot of salt. Mild white rice and brown rice vinegars are deeply aromatic and provide the perfect complement to sweet ingredients.

The spices used to create the unique flavor of Chinese food come from all corners of the world. A native of the moist jungles, pungent fresh ginger (*Zingiber officinale*) bites the tongue and awakens taste buds. Long used in Asian cooking, it was a pre-Roman import into Europe. Equally at home in curries and sweet desserts, ginger also marries well with the soft taste of rice vinegar. (For more about ginger, see pages 2–3.)

Star anise (*Illicium verum*) is the fruit of a small evergreen of the magnolia family. Grown in China and Indochina, it arrived in Europe in the late seventeenth century. Star anise is much used in pork and duck dishes and is, along with various combinations of anise, pepper, cassia, cloves, and fennel, an ingredient in the intoxicating Five Chinese Spices.

A native of India, sesame (*Sesamum indicum*) is one of the world's most important seed oils. An annual plant growing up to 6 feet tall, its seeds can be red, brown, black, or white. The seeds, lightly toasted and pressed, produce a fragrant, thick, expensive oil. This is potent stuff—a drop or two may be all you need to perfume a whole dish.

Prolific daylilies (*Hemerocallis flava*, *H. fulva*), happy immigrants that bloom cheerfully with a minimum of care, may be the most valuable herbaceous perennial ever imported from China. The ancient Chinese were well aware of its artistic merit but were more engaged by the daylily's economic and medical properties. The steamed and dried buds represented a cash crop to small farmers, and the crown and root found their way into many an herbal remedy. Known as "Yellow Flower Vegetable" or "Golden Needle Vegetable," the dried blossoms are high in Vitamin A and B as well as protein. Daylilies are the symbol of mother love, and to artist and poet they are known as "Mother Herb" or "Forget Trouble Herb."

While an elaborate New Year banquet would be expected in a Chinese household, the Chinese New Year can be welcomed somewhat more simply. The following recipes don't pretend to be authentic, but they do offer new tastes and a way to serve a quick but elegant meal. Add steamed rice and sage or Chinese dinner tea, and you'll be all set to celebrate.

Star Anise Mandarin Oranges

SERVES 4

Drain the liquid from the can of mandarin oranges into a small saucepan, heat to simmer, add 2 star anise clusters, simmer 1 minute longer, and pour over the mandarin orange sections in a covered glass container. Cover and refrigerate overnight. Serve as dessert with almond cookies or fortune cookies.

Smashed Cucumber Salad

SERVES 4

1 long greenhouse-grown cucumber, scrubbed
1 clove garlic, sliced thin
$\frac{1}{4}$-inch slice of fresh ginger root, minced fine
1 teaspoon sugar
4 tablespoons brown rice vinegar
a few drops sesame oil

Cut cucumber into $\frac{1}{4}$-inch slices and smash with a mallet or cleaver. Combine remaining ingredients and pour over cucumbers in a glass jar. Cover and refrigerate until ready to serve.

Stir-Fried Pork with Lily Buds

SERVES 4

This is equally good made with sautéed tofu (or a combination of pork and tofu).

$\frac{1}{4}$ cup daylily buds
1 teaspoon light soy sauce
2 teaspoons dry red wine
$\frac{1}{2}$ teaspoon sugar
$\frac{1}{2}$ pound lean pork, shredded
$1\frac{1}{2}$ tablespoons peanut oil
4 scallions, cut lengthwise and then diagonally in 1-inch sections

Cut the daylily buds in half and soak in water to cover for $\frac{1}{2}$ hour. Combine soy sauce, wine, and sugar in small bowl and toss with pork; allow to stand for 10 minutes. Squeeze out marinade and put aside to add to dish later. Heat wok or heavy skillet over high flame, add oil, toss in the meat, and coat each piece with oil. Continue cooking over high heat, stirring frequently, until pork loses its pinkness. Add scallions. Squeeze water from daylilies, add to pork-scallion mixture, toss, add remaining marinade, and simmer for 5 minutes. Serve over steamed rice.

Growing the
Golden Needle Vegetable

Daylilies have recently become one of the most popular plants in the garden. The prices of some of the new varieties are astronomical. For cooking, the old-fashioned lemon lily (*Hemerocallis flava*) works as well as any and is eminently affordable. The later-blooming orange lily (*H. fulva*) is also fine for cooking, but it can be a bully and prove troublesome unless planted in an area where there is lots of space for it to roam.

Daylilies can be established in naturalistic plantings and can thrive without special soil or care. They like the sun, except in the South where a little shade is welcome. Transplant or divide in the spring or after they have finished blooming.

REPUBLIC DAY
January

Cumin and Other Indian Spices

To many Americans, curry powder *is* Indian cooking, but this sometimes hot powder is strictly a European invention. Curry is, in the strictest sense, a sauce used to flavor other ingredients or to lend character to rice and chapatis. Various dried spices are toasted and then ground before being added to the other ingredients to produce an infinite variety of complexly seasoned dishes. The spices most often used in the blend we think of as curry may include black pepper, chili, cloves, cardamom, cinnamon, coriander, cumin, ginger, mustard seed, turmeric, and fenugreek. The measurements and ingredients differ from recipe to recipe.

It is difficult to imagine Indian cooking before the Portuguese importation of the chili pepper. This blazing vegetable, along with fresh ginger root, gives zing and heat to Indian food.

Cumin
Cuminum cyminum

Both are digestive stimulants, so their popularity is not surprising in countries where hot weather tends to dull appetites. With its reputation as a digestive aid, the addition of ginger to heavily spiced dishes may alleviate any distress caused by the other seasonings.

Cardamom (*Elettaria cardamomum*) and all the other members of the ginger family, including turmeric (*Curcuma longa*), are staples of Indian cooking. The tiny, ridged cumin (*Cuminum cyminum*) seed, symbol of miserliness ("he is so cheap, he would try to split a cumin seed") complements the taste of peppers and also appears often in Eastern European and Mexican cooking.

Indian cuisine also uses the musky flavor of fresh coriander (*Coriandrum sativum*) leaves and the spicy, slightly sweet orange flavor of the coriander seed. (Fresh coriander, also called cilantro or Chinese parsley, is thought by the Chinese to bestow immortality and is best used sparingly by the uninitiated. It resides in the produce department while the seeds are shelved with spices.) Pungent black mustard (*Brassica nigra*) and brown mustard (*B. juncea*) seeds are commonly used whole or lightly ground. *Kalon*, the tiny black seeds of *Nigella sativa*, are sometimes sold as onion seeds in Indian or Middle Eastern markets. They create an intriguing and exotic flavor when sprinkled on breads.

A month spent preparing Indian food for the Sage Cottage herb classes convinced me that only a country with a large population could sustain a cuisine that requires so much mashing and grinding. Still, the taste is worth the work.

On January 26, 1950, less than two years after the assassination of Mahatma Ghandi, Jawaharlal Nehru was sworn in as Prime Minister of the new Democratic Republic of India. Toast Republic Day with a glass of fruit juice or cup of strong tea and try a bit of spicy food.

Garam Masala
(Spice Mixture)

Garam Masala is an aromatic mixture of spices used in Indian recipes from stews to dried beans. The measurements and ingredients differ from family to family, from recipe to recipe, and from region to region. Even using a food processor, grinding the spices is hard work, so you might just as well make up enough to use in several dishes. Use 2 teaspoons for one batch of bulgur salad. Seal the remainder in a glass jar to use for other salads or to mix with olive oil and brush on toasted pita bread.

4 teaspoons cumin seeds
4 teaspoons coriander seeds
2 teaspoons peppercorns
1 1-inch piece stick cinnamon
1½ teaspoons cardamom seeds
½ teaspoon whole cloves

Bulgur Salad with Indian Spices
SERVES 6

2 cups bulgur
3¾ cups boiling water
1 medium onion, minced fine
2 cloves garlic, sliced fine
1 tablespoon wine vinegar
1 tablespoon olive oil
2 teaspoons Garam Masala

Add bulgur to boiling water and cook 1 minute. Cover and set aside to cool to lukewarm. In the meantime, using a mortar and pestle or spice/coffee grinder or food processor, coarsely grind together all the spices of the Garam Masala (you may also use previously ground spices). Stir onion, garlic, wine vinegar, and oil into bulgur. Toss with 2 teaspoons of the spice mixture, cover, and refrigerate. Best served at room temperature.

For variety, add 2 teaspoons of the Spice Mixture to a can of baked beans and bake (Bombay Baked Beans?) or replace the bulgur called for in the Bulgur Salad with cooked lentils and serve the dish hot.

———

Three C Salad

SERVES 6

Any attempt to find edible tomatoes in the dead of winter is bound to end with failure. There is an alternative (remember, I said alternative, not substitute). Buy any good brand of canned Italian plum tomatoes and drain the liquid; then squeeze the tomato lightly and use as you would fresh. Save the juice for soups and stews.

2 large fresh tomatoes, chopped coarsely (or 4 drained Italian plum tomatoes)
2 large green peppers, chopped fine
½ cup plain, low-fat yogurt
½ teaspoon chili powder
½ teaspoon ground cumin
¼ cup minced chives
1 teaspoon corn oil
1 tablespoon mustard seeds

Combine tomatoes and green peppers in a low glass or china bowl. Stir in yogurt and spices. Heat oil in a small skillet; add mustard seed and immediately cover (mustard seed is like popcorn and will splatter all over the kitchen if it is not contained). Shake covered pan over medium heat for several minutes, remove from heat, and stir mustard seed into tomato-pepper mixture. Stuff into toasted pita bread halves alone or with Spicy Eastern Burgers (recipe follows).

Spicy Eastern Burgers

SERVES 6

1 pound lean ground turkey
1½ cups carrots, peeled and grated
¼ cup fresh bread crumbs
1 tablespoon minced fresh coriander (cilantro)
2 hot, green chilis, diced
2 egg whites, lightly beaten
1 tablespoon minced fresh ginger
1 teaspoon ground cumin
2 cloves garlic, minced
1 tablespoon lemon juice
6 small pita breads
1 teaspoon onion seeds

Combine first ten ingredients; mix until well blended. Divide mixture into 6 portions and shape into 6 patties. Broil in the oven or over a rack on the grill.

Split 6 pitas, spread the inside very lightly with vegetable oil, and sprinkle with lightly crushed onion seeds (*Kalon*). Bake at 400° F for 4 minutes. Top 6 slices with meat patty and 2 tablespoons Three C Salad, add other half of pita and top with remaining salad.

Curry Plants

Curry is a puzzlement. Just as curry isn't really one mix, the curry plant (*Helichrysum angustifolium*) does not produce curry powder.

This ever-gray shrub grows 2 feet—as wide as it is tall. It is an appealing plant for the sunny, winter windowsill as well as an interesting touch for the summer garden. The plant resents being trimmed at the tips of the branches, so try to grow yours as a standard (a plant that is restricted to a single treelike stem, with the growth concentrated at the crown). Cut the branches off the lower part of the stem and leave the top alone. The curry plant adapts to medium-dry soil. It can be used in cooking; a sprig adds a mild, curry flavor to rice and bean dishes.

FEBRUARY

If Candlemas Day be fair and bright,
Winter will have another flight;
But if Candlemas Day be clouds and rain,
Winter is gone and will not come again.

We look to nature for signs that winter will soon break. On Candlemas (February 2), the residents of Puxatawny, Pennsylvania, watch the groundhog as avidly as the ancients watched the weather for predictions reassuring them that winter would pass quickly.

Nature writer Joseph Wood Krutch complains about the month of February: "The one we could do without. Spring is too far away to comfort by anticipation, and winter long ago lost the charm of novelty. This is the very 3 A.M. of the calendar." Perhaps that is why we take such keen pleasure in all the little holidays this shortest month affords, celebrations calculated to satisfy the belly as well as our flagging spirits.

SHROVE TUESDAY
February

Fenugreek and Breakfast Treats

Always before Lent there comes a waddling fat, grosse groome, called Shrove Tuesday, one whose manners show he is better fed than taught and indeed he is the only monster for feeding amongst all the dayes of the yeare, for he devoures more flesh in fourteen hours than this old kingdom doth (or at least should doe) in six weekes after.

— John Taylor, "Jack-a-Lent" (1630)

John Taylor (1580–1653), the eccentric "Water Poet" and pamphleteer, came down hard on the gluttony that characterized Shrove Tuesday, the day reserved for finishing up the drippings in the larder before Ash Wednesday, when the meat-free Lenten fast began. Taylor sniffs contemptuously at the use of "wheat'n flowre . . . with water, eggs, spice, and other tragical inchantments, . . . put it little by little into a fryingpan of boyling suet . . . until at last by the skill of the cooke it is transformed

Fenugreek
Trigonella foenum graecum

52

into the forme of a 'flap-jack.' " When this "sweete candied baite" was ready, a bell was rung, calling one and all to the fatty feast.

In England, it was the custom for faithful Christians to apply to a priest to be shriven (or absolved) of their sins before embarking on the six-week fast that culminated in the celebration of Easter. To this end, the shriving-bell was tolled from the church steeple to remind people of their obligation. In time, the shriving-bell and the panburn-bell or pancake bell became one and the same. Legend tells us that the custom of pancake races on Shrove Tuesday came about when a harried housewife, hearing the shriving-bell and rushing from her kitchen to church for absolution, forgot that she had a griddle in her hand. Soon others joined the race. This 500-year-old tradition continues on a transatlantic scale as house-wives from Liberal, Kansas, and Olney, England, dash 415 yards down the streets of their respective towns at the sound of the pancake bell, flipping the pancake at the beginning and end of the course. Liberal and Olney compare race time by long-distance phone, and the winner receives a "kiss of peace" and the blessing "The Peace of the Lord be alway with you."

The wildest, most uninhibited day of Carnival in Latin countries, Shrove Tuesday is celebrated in Germanic areas and the Pennsylvania Dutch region of the United States as *Fastnacht* (literally Fast or Lenten Eve). The Pennsylvania Dutch serve *fastnachts*, fried cakes or doughnuts. In Lancaster and Lebanon counties, this fried cake is sometimes split, filled with molasses, and dunked in saffron or blue balsam tea. In other places, the *fastnacht kuche* (cake) is spread with *gwidde hunnich* (quince jam) or crab apple jelly.

Even if diet or food sensitivities make you reluctant to swallow the "sweete candied baite" that is the mark of either the flapjacks or *fastnachts*, you can celebrate *Fastnacht* with these more healthful breakfast treats for your Shrove Tuesday breakfast.

You will probably be surprised to discover that the sweetly perfect flavor of real maple syrup is often imitated by fenugreek seeds (*Trigonella foenum graecum*). The tiny pillowlike seeds (thought to attract money to the house) are slightly bitter but have the scent of maple, and they are used in a delicious syrup that's just perfect for celebrating Shrove Tuesday.

—

Wholesome Whole-Grain Pancakes

SERVES 4

These good-tasting, low-cholesterol pancakes are great for the person who is allergic to whole wheat flour or milk. If whole eggs are a problem, you can substitute 2 eggs' "worth" of Ener-G egg replacer.

^{2}/$_3$ cup whole wheat flour or 1^1/$_8$ cups rolled oats whirled in a blender

^{1}/$_4$ cup coarse cornmeal

^{1}/$_3$ cup rolled oats

1 teaspoon baking powder or 1¾ teaspoons low-sodium baking powder

^{1}/$_2$ teaspoon baking soda

1^1/$_4$ (or more) cups apple juice (If you have no apple juice on hand, use 1^1/$_4$ cups water to which you have added 1^1/$_4$ teaspoons lemon juice.)

2 egg whites

1 tablespoon plus 2 teaspoons vegetable oil

1 tablespoon water

^{1}/$_2$ teaspoon vanilla

Mix together dry ingredients in a medium bowl. Combine remaining ingredients, beating lightly with a fork. Add wet ingredients to dry, stirring lightly until just combined to make a soft batter. Batter should not be too stiff. Heat a griddle over medium-high heat (400–425° F) and spray lightly with a vegetable oil spray. Pour a scant $1/4$ cup batter onto griddle for each pancake. Cook until bubbles begin to form on the top; turn and cook other side until brown. Serve with Sweet Anise Apples (recipe follows), "Maple" Apple Syrup, apple sauce, or a bit of low-calorie imitation maple syrup.

———

Sweet Anise Apples

SERVES 6–8

4 apples, quartered, cored, and thinly sliced
$1/2$ cup undiluted frozen apple juice concentrate
$1/4$ teaspoon anise seeds, crushed (in a mortar and pestle or blender)
2 teaspoons sugar or 1 envelope sugar substitute (add the sugar
   substitute with the vanilla)
$1/4$ teaspoon vanilla

Combine all ingredients except vanilla and sugar substitute (if you are using it) in a small saucepan. Cover and cook over low heat until apples are mushy, about 10 to 15 minutes. Remove from heat; then add vanilla. Serve with pancakes, over low-fat yogurt, or as a topping for toasted rice cakes.

"Maple" Apple Syrup

1½ CUPS

Fenugreek seeds are most often found in Indian cooking, but their slightly maple flavor makes them a good choice for creating artificial maple syrup.

- 1 12-ounce can frozen unsweetened apple juice concentrate
- 2 teaspoons fenugreek seeds, crushed
- 1 12-ounce juice can of water
- 1 tablespoon plus 1 teaspoon cornstarch
- 2 teaspoons lemon juice

Pour apple juice concentrate into 1-quart saucepan, add fenugreek seeds (wrapped in muslin or cheesecloth), and heat over low flame 5 minutes. Add cornstarch to empty juice can along with an ounce or so of water and stir to dissolve cornstarch. Fill can with water. Stir water/cornstarch mixture into apple juice. Cook over medium heat, stirring, until thickened and slightly clear. Remove from heat, stir in lemon juice. Store covered in the refrigerator. Remove fenugreek seeds before serving.

Fenugreek Sprouts

For an unusual salad addition, sprout some fenugreek seeds. Combine equal parts sterilized potting soil, sand, and perlite to fill a small 12x3x3-inch planter. Place planter in a pan containing warm water and allow to soak 15 or 20 minutes. Remove from water and allow to drain. Strew fenugreek seeds about $3/4$ inch apart over the surface of the soil; cover seeds with $1/8$ inch more soil. Cover planter with a piece of clear plastic until the seeds begin to sprout. When the plants reach the two-leaf stage, snip a few and toss into your salad. Or mix a few cuttings with cooked carrots and potatoes. The tangy, slightly bitter taste will perk up winter meals.

VALENTINE'S DAY
February 14

Herbs and Love Charms

While the pre-Christian origins of St. Valentine's Day are murky, man and woman's search for the perfect love potion is ancient, persistent, and creative (but alas, unsuccessful). Much of the earth's bounty—from endive to mint, burdock to houseleeks, basil to coriander— has been bruited about as being aphrodisiacal. De Gubernatis reported that endive seed, touted in Germany as a love potion, would be effective only if uprooted with a piece of gold or a stag's horn on June 24 or July 25. Yarrow, the *plumajillo* of our Southwest, was reputed to be a potent charm, but only if gathered from the grave of a young man.

Curly Endive
Cichorium Endiva

The Greeks forbade their soldiers to eat mint, "as it so excites a man to lust that it diminishes his courage." Perhaps this tradition accounts for the popularity of mint tea in many countries.

Carrots, parsnips and man-shaped ginseng have all been considered erotic. These notions sprang from the doctrine of signatures about which Robert Turner wrote: "God has imprinted in the plants, herbs and flowers as it were in hieroglyphics, the very signature of their virtue."

Coriander, symbol of concealed worth in flower lore, was a principal ingredient of *Arabian Nights'* love potions. Winter savory was said to "stir-reth him that useth it to lechery," while tender asparagus and artichokes were thought to stir up bodily lust in man or woman.

Because Aphrodite, the goddess of love, was born of the sea, all manner of finned or shelled creatures are held to be food for lovers. When lewd food is the topic, oysters invariably leap to mind, but any fish will do: The potassium and iodine in them indeed releases energy from proteins necessary for normal reproduction.

The Victorian Age ushered in a more romantic but no less confusing use of things herbal. The garden became a dictionary of love. With tussy-mussy in hand, one could express tender thoughts, even delicately erotic ones, without stirring comment. The only danger lay in the shocking disagreement between the floral "linguists," creating their manuscripts from the myths of different cultures. Basil could signify love or hate; sage, wisdom or pity; the poppy, bitterness or affection. Shed a tear for the unhappy lovers working from conflicting floral dictionaries!

Your valentine won't have any doubt about your feelings if you share a lovely, loving meal on February 14. My choice for a special dinner would be a simple meal and would borrow romantic treats from all the old herbals. Nothing sets the stage for an erotic meal better than a house where the mysterious scents of blended herbs wafting into every corner tell of pleasures to come.

A valentine dinner should be an easy meal, quick to prepare after a day's work or after you've shipped the kids off to a friend's house. A simple soup of love apples (boringly described these days as tomatoes) and basil, the Roman symbol of love, would begin the repast. To accompany the soup, I would serve a loaf of hot, crusty bread, perfumed with rosemary for remembrance and shallots "to stir men's blood." There would be a fragrant stir-fry, scented with coriander seed (remember the Arabian love potions) floating among erotic baby carrots.

A salad of curly endive, whose seeds were said to be an aphrodisiac, would glisten with a tarragon vinaigrette. And for dessert, rose cookies (for rose is an anagram of Eros, the god of love) would be served with heart-shaped bowls brimming with cool chunks of fresh pineapple, the ancient symbol of hospitality.

The table would be set with banks of candles and a sky-blue bowl of jonquils discreetly signaling "desire," entwined with ivy speaking of "undying affection." Then, before your dinner companion arrives, tuck a four-leaf clover in your shoe. It's been said that the first person you see thereafter will be your life's companion.

Eve's Love Apple Broth

SERVES 2

1 cup cider
1 cup tomato juice
$3/4$ teaspoon dried basil

Combine all ingredients in a saucepan. Heat to boiling and simmer 5 minutes. Serve hot.

Eros Bread

SERVES 2

1 small loaf French bread
1 tablespoon olive oil
$\frac{1}{2}$ cup shallots or green onions, minced
1 tablespoon fresh rosemary, minced (or 1 teaspoon dried)
several grinds of fresh pepper

Cut the top off the loaf of bread and save. Pull out the "innards," tearing into 1-inch pieces. Heat oil in small nonstick skillet; add shallots or green onions, rosemary, and pepper. Cook over low heat until shallots or green onions are soft; allow to cool slightly. Toss with torn bread. Replace bread in shell, replace top, and place on a cookie sheet. Bake for 8-10 minutes in 375° F oven.

Tarragon Vinaigrette

$\frac{1}{2}$ CUP

$\frac{1}{4}$ cup olive oil
3 tablespoons red wine vinegar
3 tablespoons water
$\frac{3}{4}$ teaspoon dried tarragon
1 tablespoon finely minced parsley
1 clove garlic, crushed
$\frac{1}{2}$ teaspoon Dijon-style mustard
pinch of brown sugar

Combine all ingredients in a blender or small bowl; blend well. Serve over well-washed curly endive tossed with celery and green pepper and garnished with spears of French endive.

———

Basil Stir-Fry

SERVES 2

Couscous, which was originally understood to mean a steamed dish popular in Morocco, is now also used as a name for the quick-cooking pasta-like substance made from semolina that is part of the dish.

$1/2$ cup couscous
1 cup water
1 tablespoon corn oil
$1/4$ pound ground sirloin
$1/2$ large green pepper, sliced
1 medium carrot, pared and cut in $1/4$-inch slices on an angle
1 medium onion, sliced thin
1 teaspoon dried basil
$1/2$ teaspoon Dijon-style mustard
2 tablespoons cider vinegar
2 handfuls washed spinach

In a small saucepan, heat water to boiling, add couscous, cover, and set aside. Add oil to wok or heavy skillet; over high heat, quickly brown meat; add peppers, carrots, and onions. Continue stirring until vegetables are slightly cooked, about 2 to 3 minutes. Add basil, mustard, and vinegar and mix thoroughly. Reduce heat to low, toss spinach on top, cover, and allow to steam 3 or 4 minutes. Serve over couscous.

Aphrodite's Cupboard

Almost 2,000 years ago, Ovid lamented, "Alas there are no herbs to cure love," but the search for herbs to enhance that sweet pleasure has been far-reaching. If you're looking to try your hand at love potions, you might want to try growing savory, reputed to have earned its name from the satyrs who found it indispensable to their activities. Nicholas Culpeper, who wrote about herbs in the seventeenth century, would have you add mustard, onion, and prickly asparagus to your garden of aphrodisiacs, for he thought they were suitable for provoking lust. Dioscorides, on the other hand, maintained that *Salvia horminum* "doth provoke to conjunction." Cumin reportedly "retains love" and, along with basil and vervain, often appeared in love potions. The Arabs were partial to cardamom, and other Mediterranean people swore by fennel.

You may not have a whole garden dedicated to Aphrodite, goddess of love, beauty, and marriage, but, whatever you grow, add it with love to the food you create, and affection will surely flourish.

A PISCEAN CELEBRATION
End of February

Special Herbs for Fish

Toward the end of February, as the days noticeably lengthen, the signs of the zodiac and the dictates of the Christian church run parallel to each other. For it is then, in the midst of Lent, when fish is the focus of many meals, that Pisceans (those born between February 19 and March 20) come into their own. The two fish that represent the constellation Pisces are, according to myth, the stars into which the well-known lovers Venus and Cupid were transformed (or perhaps the fish that carried them away) when they were fleeing Typhon, that monstrous god of wind and erupting volcanos.

Pisces thus became a symbol of lovers, and, with other creatures of the sea, fish were touted as aphrodisiacs. In astrology, Pisces is supposed to exert a malign influence over the affairs of humankind, controlling the fate of sailors and bringing storms. The Chinese believed that after death souls wandered to the rim of the world, to the edge of the abyss that is the great ocean surrounding Earth; those falling over the edge were instantly converted into fish.

Lavender
Lavandula augustifolia

The early Christian church adopted the sign of the fish as its symbol in remembrance of the five loaves and two fish with which Jesus fed the multitudes. As the church evolved, fish was the food of the forty-day Lenten fast and appeared in pious Christian households every Friday throughout the year. This dietary stricture was enforced with a vengeance. Well into the seventeenth century, in parts of Europe, a person could be hanged for eating meat on Friday.

Beyond its symbolism, fish has been used as both a seasoning and a foodstuff since earliest times. The ancient Egyptians enjoyed fresh fish on their tables; dried, salted fish was a major export product. Salted fish was used as a relish by the Greeks. The Romans fermented it to create *liquamen:* sprats or anchovies, salted and then stored in an earthen crock in the sun for several months. A favorite of the Roman chef Apicius, this fragrant mixture, said to be lightly fishy with a slightly cheesy flavor, was used to season a great variety of dishes. I've read that it can be likened in taste to *nuoc mam*, used extensively in Vietnamese cooking. Apicius favored highly seasoned fish, adding startling combinations of lovage, rue, oregano, "green coriander," savory, fennel, and laser root (perhaps *Ferula foetida*) to his dishes. It's clear that the taste of the fish itself was lost in its herbal accompaniment. Modern cooks use a gentler touch with their fish. Julia Child favors bay, a bit of thyme, and a touch of marjoram, fennel, and parsley all gentled with lots of cream and butter. At Sage Cottage, we find a touch of olive oil, a smattering of fresh herbs, and a quick sauté to bring out the flavor of the fish are a simple substitute for complicated high-cholesterol sauces.

Fennel and lavender are imaginative additions to most fish dishes. Fennel (*Foeniculum vulgare*), a tall garden perennial (albeit a short-lived one in our climate), produces both foliage and seeds with a distinctive anise scent and taste. It was one of the nine healing herbs of the Anglo-

Saxons and was included in the ninth-century garden list of Charlemagne. The seeds were thought to dull the appetite, although the use of fennel on fish certainly has the opposite effect.

Lavender, most often associated with baths and for scenting clothes, is a minute but vital ingredient in Herbes de Provence (page 108). It was also much used by the Shakers in desserts. Adding a few dried blossoms, carefully crumbled, to fish dishes creates a startling but intriguing taste.

———

Fennel Tuna with Lavender

SERVES 4

The combination of fennel and lavender, so wonderful in Herbes de Provence (page 108), makes canned tuna something special. This recipe is just the ticket for a quick-off-the-shelf dinner.

> 1 large can tuna, packed in water
> $1/2$ cup plain, low-fat yogurt
> $1/2$ teaspoon fennel seeds, crushed
> $1/8$ teaspoon dried lavender flowers
> $1/2$ teaspoon Dijon-style mustard

Drain tuna in a strainer and rinse with cold water. Place tuna in a flat broiler-proof dish, breaking it up as you do. Combine remaining ingredients and spread over tuna. Place in a 350° F oven for 10 minutes (or in a microwave at half power for 3 minutes). Stir tuna to mix yogurt sauce into it; bake an additional 8–10 minutes (or microwave on high 1 minute). Serve hot or cold.

Portuguese Fish Soup

SERVES 6

It's said that the Portuguese can prepare cod every day of the year and never repeat a recipe. Portuguese mothers are reputed to check out the codfish repertoire of their son's intended brides. This thick, easy soup would find favor with even the fussiest prospective Portuguese mother-in-law, and Apicius would have loved the combination of herbs.

1 large eggplant, peeled and cut into $\frac{1}{2}$-inch pieces
2 tablespoons olive oil
$1\frac{1}{4}$ cups coarsely chopped onions
6 cloves garlic, peeled
1 green pepper, chopped
$\frac{1}{4}$ cup water
1 teaspoon dried summer savory
$\frac{1}{2}$ teaspoon dried thyme
1 bay leaf
3 cups canned Italian plum tomatoes, broken up
2 cups water
$\frac{3}{4}$ cup rice (Basmati or another short-grain rice is nice if you have it)
$\frac{1}{2}$ teaspoon cumin seeds, crushed
$\frac{1}{2}$ teaspoon fennel seeds, crushed
$1\frac{1}{2}$ pounds fresh or frozen cod, cut in chunks

Cover eggplant pieces with cold water and allow to stand for $\frac{1}{2}$ hour; drain and pat dry. Heat oil over medium heat in a large Dutch oven; add eggplant, onions, garlic, and green pepper; stir to coat with oil. Add $\frac{1}{4}$ cup water and cook until vegetables are soft, stirring often. Add more water as necessary to prevent burning. Add savory, thyme, bay leaf, tomatoes, and 2 cups water. As soon as mixture comes to a boil, add rice and cover. Reduce heat and cook 5 minutes. Add cumin, fennel, and cod. Continue cooking until rice is tender. Fish out the garlic cloves and mash. Add 1 clove to each heated soup dish. Serve with bread sticks.

Salmon-Spinach Torte

SERVES 6

Salmon Layer

1 16-ounce can red salmon, drained
4 slices bread, cut into ¼-inch cubes
1 tablespoon lime juice
¼ cup milk
2 teaspoons Dijon-style mustard
3 tablespoons finely minced parsley

Spinach Layer

1 teaspoon corn oil
3 tablespoons finely minced shallots
1 teaspoon dried dill weed (or 1 tablespoon fresh)
1 pound spinach, heavy stems removed (or 2 packages frozen
    chopped spinach, defrosted and squeezed dry)
½ cup low-fat or nonfat cottage cheese
several grinds pepper

Break up salmon with a fork. Mix in 1 cup bread cubes, setting aside the remainder for topping. Sprinkle salmon and bread cubes with lime juice. Combine milk, mustard, and parsley; stir into salmon mixture.

Add corn oil to a small saucepan; add shallots and cook over medium heat until soft. Crumble dill over shallots, toss in spinach, cover, and cook over low heat for 4 minutes. Mix in cottage cheese and pepper.

Heat oven to 350° F. Spray 8x8-inch pan with vegetable oil. Spread half of salmon mixture in bottom, spread all the spinach mixture over that, and top with remaining salmon. Bake 15 minutes; then top with remaining bread cubes and continue baking for 10 more minutes or until cubes are brown and mixture is bubbly. Cut in squares to serve. Serve as a main dish with *ancini de pepe* pasta tossed with ¼ cup shredded carrots that have been seasoned with 1 teaspoon olive oil mixed with 1 teaspoon tarragon vinegar or carrots and parsnips steamed with thyme.

Lavender in the Garden

Lavender brings to mind lace handkerchiefs, fainting ladies, and English gardens. At Sage Cottage, we have had good luck wintering over our lavenders by providing a winter cover of pine boughs and a gravely, limey soil that drains well. *Lavandula augustifolia*, available in several varieties, is generally hardy in Zone 5. It can be started easily from seed or cuttings. If you already have several plants and covet more, this spring you might want to try covering one of your plants halfway up its height with sand. Then place a few small, flat rocks on the mound. The covered stems will root, and next spring you'll have a forest of plants. Cut the rooted stems from the mother plant and replant in a sunny location.

If you have mild winters, by all means add the finely toothed, wavy-leaved, *L. dentata* (French lavender) as well as *L. lanata* that has woollier leaves and long-stemmed, dark purple flowers.

Harvest your lavender just when the flowers start to open. If you pick heavily, you should have a second crop of flowers.

JOB'S BIRTHDAY
February 30

Dandelion and Other Lawn Edibles

Poor Job. Beset by all manner of woes, he prayed, "Let the day perish wherein I was born . . . Let it not be joined unto the days of the year, let it not come into the number of months." And to this day it hasn't. His birthday is celebrated on the thirtieth day of February.

Some modern gardeners consider Job's suffering small potatoes compared with the trials they experience eradicating weeds from their lawns. On every hand, home owners are urged to join the war on weeds to eradicate forever those interlopers that mar the green velvet of their lawns. Stop! Using those chemicals could wipe out herbs for the pot and the salad bowl, destroy teas and medicines, and pollute the ground water and atmosphere.

Dandelion
Taraxacum officinalis

On Job's birthday, while those of us in the Northeast pray for an early spring, lawns are already flourishing for our southern neighbors. They celebrate Job's birthday by getting out the lawnmower. In the Southwest, melting winter snows and warm days create lush greenery and growing lawns. If the snowcover has been light, the watering has already begun.

When you head out to give your lawn and garden their spring cleanup, sit down and really look at them. That low-growing plant with the tiny leaves and delicate white flower is chickweed (*Stellaria media*), and the clumps of arrow-shaped leaves spreading everywhere are sheep sorrel (*Rumex acetosella*). Good King Henry (*Chenopodium bonus-henricus*), Lamb's quarters (*Chenopodium album*) and orach (*Atriplex hortensis*) thrive on the unkempt lawn and add their mild, slightly bitter taste to the spring pottage. Arrow-leaved Good King Henry was grown as a potherb in England and has escaped into the wild on this continent. Succulent, dark green purslane (*Portulaca oleracea*) creeps into the flower beds. Showiest of all is the dandelion (*Taraxacum officinalis*), which brightens our spirits and lawns each spring. Cornell University's great teacher and botanist Liberty Hyde Bailey thought each dandelion blossom "worth more than a gold coin."

If you'd like to try some lawn teas, check out alehoof (*Nepeta glechoma*) with its tiny snapdragonlike spikes. Alehoof garnered its common name as a flavoring for ale, but the aromatic leaves were used by the very poor in England as tea. Dried red clover blossoms (*Trifolium pratense*), high in protein, calcium, and phosphorus, mixed with a bit of mint also make a tasty tea.

Come spring, our forebears foraged for good green things to put in the pot and for "sallets" (salads). Imagine a winter spent eating little but stored root crops and you'll understand their hunger and their bodies' need for crisp, fresh greens—greens for salads, greens for the pot, and greens from which to concoct a cellar full of wines and beers. In spite of advances in the distribution of foodstuffs, our diets today are less interesting and, to a great extent, more restricted.

Of all the greens our ancestors ate, two—sorrel and dandelion—are still generally used in the kitchen. Both are laden with vitamins and minerals and are delightful to the taste.

Rich in Vitamin A, the dandelion, or blowball, has been used as a potherb, the roots as a substitute for coffee, and the leaves when picked tiny and tender in the spring, as a zesty addition to salads. And surely, no wine cellar would be complete without dandelion wine.

Cultivated French sorrel (*Rumex scutatus*) is the best variety for culinary purposes, but our common sheep sorrel (*Rumex acetosella*) can be used in its stead. The sharp, acidic taste is said to sharpen the appetite. The high oxalic acid content of the sorrel suggests that it is best consumed in small quantities. Yellow wood sorrel (*Oxalis stricta*) with its delicate heart-shaped leaves is edible, but caution is the watchword. The oxalic acid it contains can be harmful if you eat a large quantity.

I like sorrel mixed in any fresh salad but care less for it cooked as a potherb. In soup, though, it is spring personified.

Taraxacum officinalis, blowball, the ubiquitous dandelion is yours for the picking. In Henry Ward Beecher's words, "these Golden Kisses all over the cheeks of the meadow," the bane of the lawn-proud, have been cultivated in kitchen herb gardens for centuries. Collect yours from the lawn or the produce counter and be prepared for gutsy eating. If you're foraging for them, pick only from places that haven't been treated with herbicides and collect the young leaves before flowering. And while you're at it, dig a root or two for salad.

Steam dandelion greens lightly in the water left on the leaves from washing. Serve as you would spinach or toss lightly with a tablespoon or two of Gramma Hallett's Go-with-Anything Green Dressing.

Dandelion Salad with Gramma Hallett's
Go-with-Anything Green Dressing

Dandelion salad is most often made with a warm bacon dressing. For a change, try this recipe.

Dandelion Salad   SERVES 1
$^1/_2$ cup dandelion greens
$^1/_2$ cup torn leaf lettuce
2 tablespoons sliced radishes
1 tablespoon washed and cubed dandelion root
1 tablespoon minced chives

Mix ingredients and toss with cooled Gramma Hallett's dressing to taste.

Dressing $1^1/_4$ CUPS
1 egg white
1 tablespoon margarine
1 tablespoon corn oil
$^1/_2$ cup cider vinegar
$^1/_2$ cup skim milk
1 teaspoon honey
1 teaspoon dry mustard
$^1/_2$ teaspoon celery seeds, crushed

In a small saucepan, whisk together all ingredients. Heat over very low heat, without boiling, whisking or beating while it cooks, until thickened slightly. Allow to cool and use as salad dressing. Can be stored covered in the refrigerator for up to one week. When summer comes, try it as a dressing for coleslaw. Also try it warm over wilted spinach or dandelion greens.

———

Sorrel Spinach Soup

SERVES 4

A spring tonic in a bowl, our soup recipe combines the sparky taste of sorrel with spinach for a better color—a treat for the taste and the eye. The marjoram, thyme, and basil give it extra punch.

> 1 medium carrot, potato, and onion, chopped
> 2 cloves garlic, crushed
> 3$\frac{1}{2}$–4 cups chicken or vegetable stock
> 1 package fresh spinach, washed, with large stems removed (or 1 package frozen chopped spinach)
> 6 ounces fresh sorrel, large stems removed
> 1 tablespoon corn oil
> 1 tablespoon flour
> $\frac{1}{4}$ teaspoon each dried basil, marjoram, and thyme
> 2 tablespoons thinly sliced sorrel for garnish
> $\frac{3}{4}$ cup plain, low-fat yogurt

Cover carrot, onion, potato, and garlic with 2 cups of stock; cook until tender. Add spinach and sorrel; allow to steam for 3 minutes. Puree cooled vegetables and liquid in blender or food mill.

Make a roux by adding oil to nonstick saucepan, whisk in flour, and cook over medium heat until lightly browned.

Whisk in 1½ cups of the reserved chicken stock; cook over low heat until thickened. Add spinach/sorrel mixture; stir in herbs; simmer gently over low heat for 5 minutes. If soup is too thick, add more stock.

Pour soup into heated bowls. Add a dollop of yogurt and sprinkle on the reserved sorrel. Serve with thin, Danish rye flatbread, topped with cottage cheese mixed with caraway and fennel seeds.

Some Final Words on Weeds

A word of caution: Do not harvest weeds from areas that have been treated with chemicals. For the best flavor, pick the smallest leaves you can find.

Before you join the weed war, consider Dorothy Jacob's advice in *The Witch's Guide to Gardening* (Taplinger Publishing Co., 1965): "It is wicked to hoe up weeds, as God planted them. He doesn't wish for them to be disturbed."

MARCH

March—in like a lion, out like a lamb or vice versa. March—the first month of the year on the ancient Roman calendar and the time when, according to nature writer Joseph Wood Krutch, "the calendar of the soul begins."

March lives up to the character of its namesake, Mars, the Roman god of war, for it is a month of violent weather. Never a shrinking violet, Mars chose to name the first month of his calendar for himself. Called Lectenmoanth (lengthmonth) by the Saxons, March is indeed a time of lengthening days. Tree buds swell and all growing things stand poised at the starting line, ready for the running race to fall.

Too early for any real garden work, March is a good time to check the shallow-rooted plants in the herb garden and push them gently back into the ground. Alternate freezing and thawing coupled with the winds of February and March are the bane of thymes and other plants that cling to the top of the ground.

SAINT DAVID'S DAY
March 1

All Hail the Alliums

For those of us old enough to remember, spring and the taste of leeks or wild onions are inextricably entwined. Who can forget the taste of oniony milk poured unsuspectingly over breakfast cereal? The cows, let out of the barns after a winter's confinement, were not particular over which greenery they gobbled, so we suffered for their enthusiasm.

Most alliums, if used delicately and with finesse, create subtle tastes and satisfying accents to almost any dish. The pungent leek (*Allium porrum*) was even elevated to the status of an unofficial national emblem of Wales after a memorable battle in A.D. 640. The Welsh forces under the command of Cadwalader, about to meet the Saxon forces of Edward King of North-umberland, took the advice of Saint David, future patron saint of Wales, to tuck leeks into their caps as they went into battle. The odor of the leeks helped them distinguish friend from foe, and the Welsh emerged victorious.

Leeks
Allium porrum

Soon, on Saint David's Day (March 1), Welsh mantelpieces were garlanded with the fragrant vegetable, and the Royal Welsh Fusiliers celebrated by decking their busbys with it. The tradition lingers in a more elegant though less fragrant fashion. In more recent times, gilded leeks have taken the place of fresh.

The ancient Egyptians and Chinese cultivated leeks for food. And among the Romans, Pliny tells of Nero devouring the odoriferous leek to clear his voice, a gastronomic idiosyncrasy that earned him the derisive nickname "Porrophagus" (onion eater).

John Gerard, in his sixteenth-century herbal, warned that the "leac . . . heateth the body, ingendreth naughty bloud, causeth troublesome and terrible dreams." No mention of the wonderful, slightly sweet, yet assertive taste that lends its signature to Scotch broth, cock-a-leekies, pot au feu, fish soups, and lamb dishes.

The other members of this huge family of perhaps 400 species vary in form and taste. Polite, ladylike, and ornamental chives (*Allium schoenoprasum*) and the French favorite, shallots (*A. ascalonicum*), certainly are the genteel side of the family that also boasts robust, vampire-fighting garlic (*A. sativum*) and odoriferous ramps (*A. tricoccum*).

The common onion (*Allium cepa*) is, throughout the world, the most popular seasoning. Today, its reputation as the cook's friend transcends its use over the centuries as a medicine. Onions were once hung over doors to ward off infections, and Grant's plea to Lincoln for cartloads of onions to alleviate dysentery among his troops seems quite reasonable in light of recent discoveries about their bactericidal effect. Current research also hints that the regular consumption of members of the allium family may reduce the risk of heart attack and lower serum cholesterol and blood pressure.

Leek and Cheese Pudding

SERVES 4

A quiche without a crust and with no egg yolks, this is especially tasty with a carrot salad or with steamed spinach tossed with 1 teaspoon rice vinegar. Toasted whole-wheat-bread fingers brushed with rosemary or garlic oil are nice for crunch. Leftover pudding can be eaten cold, tucked into toasted pita bread.

2 teaspoons olive oil

3 cups sliced leeks (cleaned carefully, leaving 1 inch of green on the stalks)

$1/2$ cup thinly sliced celery

$1/2$ cup chopped onion

2 cloves garlic

$1/2$ 12-ounce package frozen chopped spinach, defrosted and squeezed dry

1 bay leaf

$1/2$ teaspoon dry mustard

$1/2$ teaspoon dried rosemary

$1/8$ teaspoon ground allspice

$1/2$ teaspoon dried thyme

$1/2$ cup water

4 tablespoons sesame seeds

a shake of cayenne pepper

2 cups low-fat cottage cheese

2 teaspoons grated onion

1 large clove garlic, minced
2 tablespoons flour or potato starch
6 egg whites (or three eggs' worth of egg-free substitute)

Add oil to a large nonstick skillet; add raw vegetables and garlic. Cook over high heat, stirring constantly, for 3 minutes. Add spinach, bay leaf, mustard, rosemary, allspice, and thyme; cook 1 more minute. Add water and cook over low heat until moisture is absorbed and vegetables are tender yet crisp. Spray a shallow 2-quart ovenproof casserole with vegetable oil; sprinkle 2 tablespoons sesame seeds over the bottom and sides of the pan. Spread vegetables evenly over the bottom of the pan.

Combine cayenne, cottage cheese, grated onion, minced garlic, flour, and egg whites in the blender or food processor; blend until smooth. Pour over vegetables. Sprinkle remaining sesame seeds on top. Bake at 350° F for 25–30 minutes until the top is brown. Allow to sit 10 minutes before serving.

———

Onion Jam

6½ CUPS

Inspired by a friend's gift of Vidalia Onion Jam, we invented our own version that has become a staple at Sage Cottage. While onions may sound a bit off-putting for breakfast, this is grand on toasted whole wheat English muffins spread with yogurt cheese, spread lightly on an egg-white omelet, or mixed with a bit of cottage cheese for a tangy salad. Be careful—it can be addictive!

7 cups very thinly sliced onions
1 tablespoon olive oil
$^3/_4$ cup wine vinegar
$^1/_4$ teaspoon dried thyme
$^1/_4$ teaspoon cut up hot, dried, Chinese red pepper
$^1/_4$ teaspoon freshly ground pepper
3$^1/_2$ cups sugar
1 package Sure-Jell Light (not regular Sure-Jell)

Place onions in a bowl and cover with cold water. Allow to stand 15 minutes. Pour off the water and squeeze the onions. Repeat.

Add olive oil to a large nonstick skillet over medium heat, pour in onions, and toss with oil. Add vinegar, turn heat to low, and cover. Cook, stirring frequently, for at least 20 minutes. The onions should be soft and golden brown. If the liquid evaporates too rapidly, add a tablespoon of water as needed. Add thyme, red pepper, and black pepper, and whirl onion mixture in a blender or food processor.

Measure out 5 cups of cooked onion mixture. If you're short, you can make up the difference with a little water. Now follow the directions on the Sure-Jell Light package for peach jam, using the onion mixture and 3$^1/_2$ cups sugar.

Tips on Choosing and Preparing

When purchasing leeks, look for ones that are crisp, have a lot of white in relation to the green stems, and have their roots still attached. Fresh leeks are a must; old ones have a bitter, somewhat acrid taste. Careful cleaning is essential. This is simplified if you cut off most of the green (leave about 1 inch) and then separate the leaves under running water, letting the water run from the white to green parts. If they are going to be chopped, it's easy to slice the stem lengthwise, wash the grit out under water, and then drain carefully.

Onions should be firm, dry and unsprouted. Buy your onions individually rather than prebagged—you'll save money in the long run.

INTERNATIONAL WORKING WOMAN'S DAY

Second Week in March

Garlic

Someone, somewhere has seen fit to declare a time during the second week in March "International Working Woman's Day." Since most women work either at home or elsewhere, it is a day to honor every working woman, especially those who do more than one job. The idea is commendable, but a bit of help for the remaining 364 days would be even better. Studies show that even women with responsibilities outside the home are the household members most likely to perform the majority of household tasks. In addition, the research reveals that full-time homemakers put in hours that would horrify the average hourly employee.

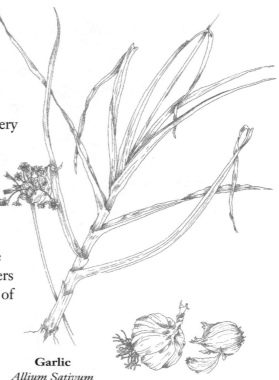

Garlic
Allium Sativum

A helpful option for working women is to shop once for the week, prepare several different dishes on Saturday, and then enjoy them for weeknight dinners with a minimum of fuss. The following meals are infinitely expandable, and their preparation includes tasks everyone in the family can do. Spread the work around and make meal preparation quality family time instead of drudgery. With a little practice, you can come up with your own collection of once-a-week-cooking meals.

The secret to this approach is organization; the magic is herbs. Sweet basil, redolent of the Mediterranean; oregano; hot, spicy chili; courageous and beneficent sage—all conspire to give mild-mannered ground turkey a bit of zing and lots of variety. You can also substitute lean ground beef or pork. And garlic is essential.

All the following recipes serve two people, so just multiply that by the number you want to serve. When cooking several meals from one recipe, garlic adds a common bass note amplified infinitely by the other ingredients.

Lloyd Harris wrote in *Time* magazine, "There's something about garlic that creates excitement." Often maligned, garlic (*Allium sativum*) is the most versatile of herbs. Once considered a panacea for all manner of ailments, garlic has been proven to have a decided effect on the body, lowering cholesterol.

As any alliumophile can tell you, the way garlic is prepared has great effect on the final taste of the dish. Used whole, the taste is mild; peeled and mashed, a bit stronger; and so on through slicing and mincing. (Marcella Hazen declared that the garlic press has no place in the kitchen of the careful cook.)

Shopping List

1 16-ounce can and 1 8-ounce
    can tomato sauce
2 pounds lean ground turkey
    (or beef or pork)
1 large egg
2 medium onions
loaf of whole wheat bread
1 cello package fresh spinach
Parmesan cheese
1 lemon
4 apples

celery
1 pound carrots
$\frac{1}{2}$ pound bulgur
$\frac{1}{2}$ pound couscous
noodles
apple juice
yogurt
1 small can mandarin
    oranges
1 fresh orange
fresh parsley

———

On Hand

basil
oregano
sage
garlic
chili powder
black pepper
thyme

fresh ginger
olive oil
wine vinegar
garlic
fennel seed
dried tarragon

The Meat

Mix up the meat for all the meals at once, adding different seasonings to each section. Then all the differently seasoned meats are cooked in one pan.

1 cup tomato sauce

1 egg white

1 tablespoon water

1 medium onion, chopped fine (save the other onion on your
   shopping list for the stir-fry)

2 cloves garlic, mashed

$1/4$ teaspoon black pepper

2 cups whole-wheat bread crumbs (let the bread dry out a little,
   then whirl in the blender or food processor)

1 cup grated carrots, packed firmly in the cup

2 pounds ground turkey

Measure tomato sauce, egg white, water, onion, garlic, pepper, bread crumbs, and carrots into a bowl. Mix lightly with fork until well blended. Add turkey and mix with your hands until blended. Divide turkey into three parts.

Meat Loaf Shape into oblong loaf (3x6 inches is about right) and place in 8$1/2$x11-inch pan. Score the top of the meat loaf in 1-inch sections. Mix $1/4$ cup of the tomato sauce with $1/2$ teaspoon chili powder, $1/4$ teaspoon each dried thyme, oregano, and grated lemon rind. Spread tomato mixture over the top of the meat loaf.

Patties Divide this part of mixture in half. Mix 1 teaspoon rubbed sage, ¼ teaspoon ground dried thyme, ½ teaspoon fresh rosemary, and 1 tablespoon fresh parsley into one part. To the other part add 1 teaspoon vinegar and ½ teaspoon grated fresh ginger. Shape each half of the mixture into two patties; place in pan with meat loaf.

Easy Oven Apples Since the oven is on, you may as well make use of it to make tonight's dessert. Slice 2 apples very thin and place in a single layer on a 12-inch square of foil, sprinkle with 1 teaspoon sugar and a dash of mace. Fold the foil around the apples into a packet and seal edges tightly.

Place meat loaf and patties in 375° F oven along with apple slices. Bake for 15 to 20 minutes.

Meatballs To remaining third of mixture, add ½ teaspoon dried basil, ½ teaspoon dried oregano, 1 tablespoon Parmesan cheese, 2 tablespoons minced parsley, 1 clove minced garlic, and ¼ teaspoon crushed fennel seeds. Mix together and shape into 12 meatballs. Set aside.

Meal 1:

Meat patties with parsleyed bulgur, spinach, carrot and celery sticks, baked apple slices

While the meat is cooking, bring 1½ cups water to a boil. Stir in ¾ cup bulgur, 1 cup fresh spinach, shredded, and ½ teaspoon dry tarragon. Allow to boil 1 minute. Cover and turn off heat. It will be ready to eat when the meat patties are done. Make carrot and celery sticks; mince parsley.

After 15 minutes, remove all meat patties from pan. Wrap ginger patties in foil and refrigerate. Top bulgur with 2 sage patties, spoon pan juice over all, and they're ready to eat with carrot and celery sticks. Before you sit down, put the meatballs into the pan with the meat loaf and return to the oven to cook for 20–25 more minutes. The apples will be done when you're ready for dessert.

After you've enjoyed your dinner, remove meat loaf, wrap in foil, and spoon meatballs into covered container. Refrigerate both. Add $\frac{1}{4}$ cup apple juice to pan drippings, scraping to remove all the goodies in the pan. Pour into a jar and refrigerate.

Now your meat for the week is all set, and you can eat the meals in any order you choose.

Meal 2:

Spaghetti and meatballs with tomato sauce and tossed spinach salad

1 tablespoon olive oil
1 clove garlic, minced
$1\frac{1}{2}$ cups tomato sauce
$\frac{1}{2}$ cup water
$\frac{3}{4}$ teaspoon dried basil
$\frac{3}{4}$ teaspoon dried oregano
6 ounces thin spaghetti
meatballs
Parmesan cheese

Add oil and garlic to saucepan over medium heat and cook until garlic is clear. Add rest of ingredients except spaghetti, meatballs, and cheese. Bring to a boil and add spaghetti broken into 3- or 4-inch pieces. After it comes to a boil again, lower heat, cover, and cook over low heat for 15 minutes. Stir mixture carefully from bottom of pan to prevent sticking.

Add meatballs, cover, and cook 10 more minutes until meatballs are heated through. Top meatballs and spaghetti with cheese; serve with green salad.

Meal 3:

Stir-fry with couscous, icy mandarin orange slices

Place can of mandarin oranges in the freezer for 20 to 30 minutes. Couscous is quicker than rice and is wonderful for sopping up the juices from a stirfry. Pour 1 cup boiling water over $1/2$ cup couscous, cover, and set aside. Slice remaining onion, shred $1^1/2$ cups of spinach, 1 cup celery and mince 1 clove garlic. Heat 1 tablespoon vegetable oil in saucepan or wok; add garlic, a thin sliver of fresh ginger, and crumbled ginger meat patty. Cook over high heat for 3 minutes; then stir in 1 tablespoon wine vinegar. Add onion, spinach, and celery; cook, tossing lightly, for another 3 minutes. Serve over couscous with an apple juice appetizer and icy mandarin oranges for dessert.

Meals 4 and 5:

Ground Lean Meatloaf with basil carrots, noodles with grated orange rind and poppy seeds, and fresh apple for dessert

Ground Lean Meatloaf sandwiches with carrot salad, apple juice

Peel and slice carrots (1 per person), cook, and toss with $1/2$ teaspoon dried basil. Pour reserved drippings from meat pan into nonstick skillet. Slice half the meat loaf into 4 pieces and add to pan. Cover and simmer gently until meat loaf is heated through. Be careful not to boil to avoid a leftover taste. Cook noodles, drain; toss with $1/4$ teaspoon grated orange rind and 1 teaspoon poppy seeds. Serve remaining meat loaf in sandwiches made with the whole wheat bread. Leftover carrots can be tossed with 1 teaspoon olive oil, 2 teaspoons wine vinegar and 1 tablespoon yogurt for a quick salad.

The Refrigerator Garden

Even if you're too busy to plant an herb garden, you can still cook with fresh herbs. Explore your local farmer's market, specialty produce shop, or the produce section of the grocery store for fresh herbs. More and more places are carrying herbs in cellophane packages. Choose bunches or packages with perfect leaves that retain a good green color and look crisp and fresh. For the best flavor, use within three or four days. For those with roots still attached (coriander is often sold this way), tuck the roots into water to cover, cover leaves with plastic, and store in the refrigerator.

To keep your parsley fresh and green, cut about $\frac{1}{2}$ inch off the stems. Remove the rubber band or string and place the stems in an inch of water in a glass. Cover with a plastic bag and store in the refrigerator. Every couple of days recut the stems, change the water, and pick off any yellowing leaves. You can also simply rinse off the parsley, shake dry, and store in a plastic bag in the refrigerator.

SAINT PATRICK'S DAY
March 17

Parsley

Even though little is known about this greenest of saints, in every corner of the world where Irish congregate Saint Patrick is honored on March 17. Statesman and priest, he clearly understood the need to adapt local superstition to the teachings of the Christian church. As he traveled throughout Ireland, the native shamrock, with three leaves on a single stem, became his way to teach the "heathen" about the Trinity. That he is supposed to have driven the snakes and vermin from the land with his hazel rod is less impressive than the documented fact that he established monasteries and schools in every corner of the Emerald Isle.

    The first recorded celebration of Saint Patrick's Day in the United States was sponsored by the Charitable Irish Society (a Protestant group) and held in Boston in 1737. Somewhat later, the first New York City Saint Paddy's

Italian Parsley
Petroselinum crispum neopolitanum

Day parade was conceived to send a clear message to the Ku Klux Klan and other anti-Irish groups of the strength of this immigrant group.

Hallmarks of the American celebration seem to be corned beef, cabbage, and green beer—all consumed while "wearin' o' the green." This year, honor St. Patrick with a fragrant green—parsley.

Ancient Greek gardens were bordered with parsley and rue, and from the Greeks comes the saying, "We are at the parsley and rue," to signify a beginning. Greek gods pastured their steeds in fields of parsley to keep them swift and spirited. The poet Homer decorated his festive tables with roses and parsley.

Parsley is available inexpensively year-round, so there's no reason to use the dried kind. (For tips on keeping parsley fresh, see page 91.) Called by some "nature's vitamin pill," parsley supplies calcium, phosphorus, and Vitamin A, adding more than decoration to your food. Finely minced, a tablespoon of fresh parsley rubbed together with any dried herb serves to freshen the taste of the dried. Even dried tarragon takes on new life when treated this way.

You know about the "wearin' o' the green" for Saint Patrick's Day, but have you ever heard of the "eatin' o' the green"? In parts of Germany, Maundy Thursday (the day before Good Friday), was called Gründonnerstag (Green Thursday) when, according to old Saxon tradition, anyone who refused to eat a green salad was in danger of becoming an ass. This year, lest you take on an asslike countenance, enjoy from Saint Patrick's Day until Easter the newly emerging parsley sprouts from last year's plants before they go to seed.

Patrick's Parsley Pasta

SERVES 6

With some cottage cheese on the side and carrot and green pepper strips on the plate rim, this makes a lovely supper. Leftovers are good served cold or at room temperature with cold corned beef.

2 large cloves garlic, sliced thin

$^3/_4$ cup finely minced Italian parsley (This amount is all of a good-sized bunch, stems removed and saved for soup or stock.)

$1^1/_2$ teaspoons dried marjoram (or 1 tablespoon minced fresh)

1 teaspoon dried basil (or 1 tablespoon minced fresh)

1 teaspoon brown sugar

$^1/_4$ cup red wine vinegar

$^3/_4$ teaspoon dry mustard

$^1/_2$ teaspoon celery seeds, crushed

2 egg whites

2 teaspoons olive oil

2 tablespoons lemon juice

freshly ground pepper

$^1/_2$ cup fresh grated Romano cheese

1 pound spiral pasta, rotelli, etc. (the more nooks and crannies, the more sauce it will hold)

Place garlic and parsley in a small bowl. Beat in herbs, brown sugar, vinegar, mustard, celery seeds, egg whites, oil, lemon juice, and pepper. Add grated cheese and mix thoroughly. Allow to stand at room temperature while you cook 1 pound spiral pasta according to package directions.

Drain and return to pot; toss with parsley and cheese mixture. Serve immediately with extra freshly grated cheese.

———

Vegetable Stock

4½–5 CUPS

Creating a rich soup stock without bones is always a challenge. If you oven "fry" the vegetables and add lots of parsley, you can succeed nicely.

>   2 tablespoons olive oil
>   4 4-inch sprigs lovage (or 4 stalks celery, sliced)
>   3 leeks, chopped (or 1 medium onion, sliced, and 2 shallots, chopped)
>   1 potato, diced
>   2 bay leaves
>   1½ cups coarsely chopped parsley
>   12 whole black peppercorns
>   6 cups water

Add olive oil to a large Dutch oven. Place in a 400° F oven for 5 minutes. Dump all the remaining ingredients, except the water, in the pan, stir to coat with oil, and return to oven. Bake for 10 minutes, stirring once. Remove from oven, add 1 cup of the water, stirring to loosen any browned vegetables from bottom of pan. Add remaining water, cover, and cook on top of stove over low heat for 1½ hours. The stock should be kept simmering. Remove from heat and strain, pressing as much liquid as possible from the vegetables. For a thicker stock, press it through a food mill. Pour into 1-pint containers and freeze for use as needed.

Parsley Soup

SERVES 4

1 tablespoon corn (or canola) oil

2 cups minced parsley

3 whole cloves garlic (Poke a toothpick through each so that you
can retrieve them when the soup is done.)

2 tablespoons sesame seeds, crushed

$\frac{1}{4}$ teaspoon chili powder

$\frac{1}{4}$ teaspoon dried thyme

4 teaspoons flour

2 cups vegetable stock (or 2 cups water mixed with $1\frac{1}{2}$ tablespoons brewer's yeast extract or 3 tablespoons brewer's
yeast flakes)

2 cups skim milk

freshly ground black pepper

2 tablespoons minced chives or green onions

Heat oil in a $1\frac{1}{2}$-quart saucepan; add parsley, garlic, sesame seeds, and
chili powder. Cook over medium heat, stirring constantly until garlic is
clear. Sprinkle thyme and flour over mixture in pan; stir to mix thoroughly.
Slowly add stock while stirring continuously; allow to cook until slightly
thickened. Stir in milk. Heat but do not boil. Pour into four heated soup
bowls, grind pepper over each serving, and garnish with chives or green
onions. Serve with toasted pita bread brushed lightly with Rosemary Oil
(page 36) and topped with a dash of grated Romano cheese. Carrot curls
add crunch and color.

Seven Times to the Devil

In the spring, no plant is more eager than parsley (*Petroselinum crispum*) to strut its stuff. A biennial, last year's parsley greens up early in the spring for a final burst of glory before going to seed.

Said to go seven or even nine times to the devil before sprouting, parsley sprouts slowly. You can sow it in March indoors in deep pots (its long taproot needs room to grow) or sow it outside around the old plants when the weather gets warmer.

When choosing seeds or cut parsley in the store, opt for the Italian variety with smooth leaves, as it has a more delicate flavor than the curly. Seedlings must be transplanted carefully to avoid shock to their long roots.

RITES OF SPRING
March

Herbs for Eggs

Since the dawn of time, eggs have been associated with new beginnings and have figured prominently in fertility rites, both human and agricultural. The Persians believed the earth was hatched from a cosmic egg, a notion shared in Egypt, Greece, and Phoenicia. The egg, symbol of earth and life, was thought to be the seat of the soul.

Dill
Anethum graveolens

Ancient Romans carefully destroyed the shells of the eggs they had eaten to save themselves from harm by the evil magic that might be worked with them. At one time, oomancy, divination by egg whites dropped in water (the shape foretelling the future), was practiced. In some parts of Europe, dreams about eggs were supposed to bring good luck; to black Southerners, broken-egg dreams presaged a quarrel. Germans and Slavs smeared a mixture of eggs, bread, and flour on their plows on Maundy Thursday to ensure a bountiful harvest. In the Maori culture, eggs were broken over the doorway of brides as they entered their homes for the first time to ensure happy marriages.

Eggs, dyed red, were an early Christian emblem of the resurrection, and throughout the world colored eggs are a symbol of spring. Parsees exchanged them; Moravians scratched white designs onto purple eggs symbolizing the joy and holiness of the Easter season; and Ukrainians created glowing *pysanky*, bright with color and alive with symbolic designs.

For all its importance in various mythologies, the "incredible, edible egg" has, of late, weathered bad press for its high cholesterol content. Rather than use the frozen, cholesterol-free egg mixtures from the store, it's less expensive to create your own. Egg whites, with a teaspoon of oil added for each egg, create fluffy omelets. With two egg whites and oil replacing each egg, you can make light, tender cakes. Your dog will enjoy the leftover yolks (his metabolism is different from yours, so they won't clog his arteries). For those who can't eat any part of the egg, it is possible to buy egg replacers (usually available in health food stores).

Basil (*Ocimum basilicum*), which literally translated from the Greek *basilikon* means "king," is one of the finest partners for eggs. To my taste, dried basil works better here than fresh basil does. Also good with apples, it truly is a royal herb.

Hot, pungent mustard, lamented by herbalist John Parkinson (1640) as the "clownes sauce" and unfit for the tables of gentlemen, enhances the taste of eggs and is the perfect partner for fish and salad dressings. Once sold only in the form of dry balls, prepared mustard is an example of early feminine enterprise. A certain Mrs. Clements of Durham, England, developed a method for making mustard flour; she then created Durham Mustard and a tidy business for herself.

Dill weed (*Anethum graveolens*), "that hindereth the witches at their will" and "stays the Hickets [hiccups]," couples well with eggs, too, especially when you grind it up with some lightly toasted sesame seeds. The dill seeds are a satisfying nibble, a dieter's delight, reminding us that they were once used to quell the hunger pangs engendered by long church services.

———

Basil Puff

SERVES 4

Reminiscent of old-fashioned popovers, this dish stretches 6 eggs to feed four people, so it's economical as well as healthful.

½ cup unbleached flour
½ cup skim milk
6 egg whites, lightly beaten
2 teaspoons corn oil
1 teaspoon dried basil (or 1¼ teaspoons dried dill weed)
grind of black pepper
2 teaspoons butter
4 teaspoons grated Parmesan cheese
chive blossoms for garnish

Preheat oven to 425° F. Position rack in center of oven. Whisk first 6 ingredients together until just combined. Place four 8–10-ounce soufflé dishes or custard cups in the oven for 2 minutes. Add ½ teaspoon butter to each heated cup and return to oven; continue heating for 2 more minutes.

Quickly divide batter evenly among the four dishes; sprinkle the top of each with 1 teaspoon parmesan cheese.

Bake 15–20 minutes, until puffy and brown. Serve immediately, garnished with chive blossoms.

———

Oven Omelet

SERVES 6

This is a good company dish. It can be prepared ahead and left in the refrigerator and then cooked and served right from the oven. This is another dish that produces spectacular cold leftovers. It can be reheated in a microwave oven but won't puff up to its former glory.

2 tablespoons olive oil
$\frac{1}{2}$ cup chopped red bell pepper
$\frac{1}{2}$ cup chopped green bell pepper
$\frac{1}{2}$ cup julienned sorrel (or fresh spinach)
1 tablespoon water
$\frac{1}{2}$ cup sliced scallions or green onions ($\frac{1}{4}$-inch slices)
$\frac{1}{2}$ teaspoon dill seeds, crushed
$\frac{1}{4}$ teaspoon black pepper
3 large eggs
6 egg whites
$\frac{1}{3}$ cup plain yogurt
$\frac{1}{3}$ cup skim milk
1 tablespoon flour

Heat oil in a nonstick skillet; then add vegetables. Stir and cook over medium heat 5 minutes. Add water, reduce heat to low, cover, and cook another 5 minutes. Stir in green onions, dill seed, and pepper. Spray 6½x10½-inch pan with vegetable oil spray; spread vegetables evenly over bottom of pan. Beat eggs, egg whites, yogurt, milk, and flour together; pour over vegetables in the pan. Bake at 425° F for 20 minutes. Serve with salsa and toasted tortillas.

Growing Dill

Dill can be easily grown from seed. Begin sowing dill in the early spring where you want it to grow, as it has a long taproot that resents transplanting. At Sage Cottage, we sow a new batch every few weeks, always being sure to plant it away from the fennel. The two are simply not compatible, and a close association will alter the taste of both.

If dill is treated to a rich soil, it should self-sow without any problem. When thinning your dill patch, toss the unwanted seedlings (minus their roots) into potato or green salad or over broiled fish.

APRIL

Whether you agree with T. S. Eliot, who calls it "the cruelest month" or with Christopher Morley's more optimistic view that "April prepares her green traffic light and the World thinks Go," the color of April is green.

Hillsides and fields are a patchwork of greens so varied that it would strain the palette of a master artist to capture the hues. The world is fresh and bright and promising.

April's name is derived from the Latin *aperire*, meaning "to open," and is dedicated to Aphrodite, the goddess of budding beauties. The siren song of April tempts us into the garden much too soon. Late starters like butterfly weed will prosper if you restrain your digging proclivities. Spend your time cleaning up the winter accumulation of debris. Let the garden rest a bit longer.

APRIL FOOL'S DAY
April 1

Savory and Other Substitutes

It is a thing to be disputed,
Which is the greatest fool reputed,
The man who innocently went
Or he that him designedly sent.

—Robert Herrick, *Poor Robin's*
    Almanac (1728)

Salt in the sugar bowl. Prince Albert in a can. A
search for the history of Eve's grandmother.
April 1 is the day to play practical jokes on family and friends, a day to send unwitting souls on
fools' errands. In Scotland, this bit of foolishness is
called Hunting the Gowk. The gowk (or cuckoo) is
the fool who is sent ever farther afield, seeking the
unfindable. In Hindustan, on the feast of Huli (March
31), the unsuspecting are sent on missions that are sure
to end in disappointment.

No records exist to explain why the first day of
April is the province of the prankster. Some say that
the custom arose to commemorate the day that Noah

Summer Savory
Satureja hortensis

104

mistakenly sent the dove from the ark to find land before the flood waters had receded.

A more likely explanation comes to us from France. Before 1564, when the New Year started on March 25, Twelfth Night fell on the first of April and was the occasion of gift-giving and feasting in France. When the calendar changed, mock gifts were presented to confuse those who forgot the new calendar. In France, the April fool is called *poisson d'Avril*, or "April fish," one that is easily hooked.

The custom of spring tomfoolery is worldwide, suggesting perhaps that the silliness arises from man's delight and giddiness over the lengthening days and promise of good weather—an outlet for spirits too long cooped up in winter quarters.

This year, don't send your family after hen's teeth or pigeon's milk. Fool them with food. The following food fakes are designed to deceive the eye while creating a more healthful diet for those around you.

Salt. Salt will hardly be missed if you add an extra helping of the traditional salt substitute, savory, to your cooking. Dill, garlic, fresh ginger, vinegar, or fresh lime or lemon all add the same sort of brightness to food that we have come to expect from salt. Fresh garlic adds a depth of flavor to salads and cooked food.

• You can, when following recipes calling for salt, eliminate the salt and add a quarter more of each herb than the amount called for.

• Herb vinegars offer an easy way to perk up the taste of everything. Add 1 tablespoon of pickling spice to warm, brown rice vinegar, allow to steep, and serve with fish. A tablespoon of garlic-basil red wine vinegar, even if you have to make do with dried basil, adds savor to the water for cooking pasta and eliminates the need for salt.

The American Heart Association and most cookbooks published about salt-free cooking offer recipes for all-purpose seasoning mixtures to replace sodium in your cooking while still retaining taste. If you currently have a favorite among these mixtures that contains either onion or garlic powder, you may find the following suggestion is a fresher-tasting seasoning mixture. Mash the herbs called for in your recipe with a teaspoon of fresh parsley; then add fresh grated onion and minced garlic to the dish.

Soy sauces. To enjoy the distinctive taste of soy sauce without so much sodium, look for a light soy sauce with the lowest sodium content; then dilute with red wine—2 parts wine to 1 part soy sauce—for a tasty addition to any stir-fry. To make your own mock soy sauce, try the recipe in this section (page 107).

Vegetable stocks take on new vigor when enhanced with 1 teaspoon brewer's yeast extract or 2 tablespoons brewer's yeast flakes for each cup of cooked liquid.

After you've purchased the leanest cuts of meat, removed the visible fat, skinned your chicken, and skimmed your soup stock, you can further reduce fat and cholesterol intake by sautéing your food over medium heat in a nonstick skillet, adding just a teaspoon or so of water to prevent burning. Add more water as necessary. Vegetables cooked this way develop a lovely, rich, caramelized taste, reducing the need for extra salt.

Cream. While nothing quite takes the place of real whipped cream on strawberry shortcake, there are two ways to mix "whipped cream" into other desserts:

• Canned evaporated skim milk chilled and freshened with a little vanilla (or nonfat milk powder mixed with half the usual water plus 1 teaspoon lemon juice) can be whipped like cream and is fine in desserts.

- Lovely, creamy soups can be concocted with evaporated skim milk.

- You'll never miss the sour cream in cooked foods if you use yogurt to which you've added ½ teaspoon cornstarch per cup, but remember, *never* boil!

- For topping baked potatoes, use plain yogurt mixed with chives (or combine ½ cup yogurt, 1 teaspoon lemon juice, and ½ cup low-fat cottage cheese; blend until creamy). For a great dip add 1 teaspoon of our Herbes de Provence to this mixture.

Mock Soy Sauce

SCANT ¼ CUP

3 tablespoons brown rice vinegar
1 teaspoon dark molasses
1 teaspoon grated onion
½ teaspoon minced garlic

Combine ingredients and store in refrigerator.

Mock Mayonnaise

1 1/4 CUPS

1 cup low-fat cottage cheese
1 tablespoon lemon juice
1/2 teaspoon dry mustard
1/4 teaspoon dried tarragon
1/2 teaspoon minced fresh lovage (or 1/4 teaspoon crushed celery
    seeds)
1 teaspoon frozen apple juice concentrate

Combine all ingredients in the container of a blender or food processor. Blend until smooth. Store in refrigerator.

─────

Herbes de Provence

1/3 CUP

Expensive to buy in the stores, this is easy to make at home. Use dried herbs.

3 tablespoons each dried marjoram and thyme
2 tablespoons dried summer savory
1 1/2 teaspoons dried rosemary
1/2 teaspoon each dried sage, dried mint, and fennel seeds
1/4 teaspoon dried lavender flowers

Combine all ingredients and store covered in jar. Crush in a mortar with pestle before using.

More Palate Teasers

Once you've started to make substitutions to improve your family's diet and fool their palates, the possibilities are endless. Salt-free tomato paste mixed with four times as much water can be substituted for sodium-packed tomato juice in cooking. Undiluted, it can be worked into casserole dishes and soups for added flavor. Shredded carrots mixed with an equal quantity of ground meat create juicy burgers and meat loaves. Undiluted frozen juice concentrates (pineapple, orange, or apple) can replace sugar in many recipes; defrosted concentrates make good toppings for yogurt or pancakes. Sugar calories may not be reduced substantially, but you'll be adding nutrients— not the empty calories of refined sugar. This is probably a more effective strategy than using honey. In most recipes, 2 egg whites plus 1 teaspoon oil can replace 1 egg, or you can use an egg replacer sold in health-food stores. Experiment with your own heathful substitutions. Join the fun— fool the family for their own good.

THOMAS JEFFERSON'S BIRTHDAY

April 13

Herbs to Enhance Spring Vegetables

Gather round ye cooks and herb fanciers! Let us toast the natal day of Thomas Jefferson. The future president was born on the thirteenth of April in the year 1743. He is my personal choice for unofficial patron saint of good food and good gardening. Whether he was busy being president, diplomat, or lawyer, come spring his thoughts turned to planting. Farming and the development of Monticello, his estate on the mountainside in Virginia, engaged his attention for sixty years.

Though a practical man, his design for the gardens and landscape at Monticello contained all the elements of the romantic landscapes then so popular in England. Jefferson's meticulous record-keeping acquaints us with the produce of his fields and the meals served at his table. He was enchanted with the preparation and presentation of food. He introduced vanilla and macaroni to the United States, and we know that as he prepared to leave Paris

Asparagus
Asparagus officinalis

at the end of his ambassadorship, he sent his steward, Adrien Petit, scurrying about town to find good olive oil, tarragon vinegar, and pasta to be sent back to Virginia. Written two days before his death in 1826, a note in his journal reveals his quandary about whether vanilla or sweet almond were the "best flavors for a blanc manger."

Wresting a productive garden from his hillside was not an easy task, as the notes from his Garden Book *Kalendar for 1809* show. The tarragon failed, the early cabbage and broccoli "failed nearly," as did the radishes, carrots, lettuce, beets, eggplant, sorrel, and okra. The Windsor beans were "killed by bugs." A discouraging year indeed for a man trying to feed a huge staff and a steady stream of guests on the produce from his kitchen garden.

Had Jefferson's vegetable crops survived that year, he might have enjoyed the bouquet of Herbly Steamed Vegetables (page 113). Each vegetable is anointed with its own herb, creating separate tastes in a haunting combination.

Lending its warm fragrance to the cauliflower, we have sweet bay (*Laurus nobilus*), about which John Parkinson wrote in his huge *Theatrum Botanicum*, "The leaves boiled in fish broth, give a fine rellish, both to meate and broth, and helpeth warme the stomake and cause digestion, without fear of casting."

Basil, whose spicy fragrance "doth make men merrie," gives a boost to pedestrian carrots, and green beans come alive with the unexpected combination of rosemary and oregano.

For asparagus, which, according to Charles Lamb, "inspires gentle thoughts," we have the dragon of the garden, tarragon. Peas and pea pods, even when not cooked "wilty," perk up with a little chive and a sprig of spearmint, appreciated by Pliny for its ability to stir "up the mind and appetite to a greedy desire for food."

Wilty Greens and Pease *(revised)*

SERVES 4–6

In his notebooks, Jefferson records his recipe for "wilty greens and pease," which (even without the cup of heavy cream called for in his original formula) takes frozen peas several steps beyond being merely edible and make fresh ones ambrosial.

$\frac{1}{4}$ cup chicken stock
$1\frac{1}{4}$ pounds fresh peas, shelled (or 1 package frozen)
6 ounces Bibb or Boston lettuce, cut in 2-inch pieces
2 tablespoons minced chives (or finely cut scallion tops)
1 teaspoon butter
freshly ground pepper
mint sprigs for garnish

Place stock in bottom of small saucepan. Add peas, lettuce, and chives; cover and cook over low heat until peas are tender. Add butter and several grinds of pepper; garnish with a sprig of mint. This is a wonderful companion to Chicken Sesame (page 143) or broiled fish.

Herbly Steamed Vegetables

1¾ CUPS PER PERSON

The vegetables you choose can change with availability, but remember to vary colors and textures. You'll need at least 2 cups of prepared veggies for each person. Those, combined with a baked potato topped with a helping of low-fat cottage cheese garnished with chives, will make a meal that sings with spring's clear voice.

Steaming is quick and easy. Add about ¾ inch water to a large skillet or pan with a tight-fitting lid; place rack or steamer in the pan and spread vegetables on the steamer; top each with the prescribed herbs, turn heat to high, and cover. Check after 5 minutes and taste-test for doneness. Jefferson's suggestion to cook asparagus only "till the head glistens jade" is good advice. When the vegetables are done to your liking, remove to a heated platter. Add 1 teaspoon butter to the remaining water in the pan and cook down until about ¼ cup remains; pour over steamed vegetables and serve.

Broccoli   Cut off the florets and save for a stir-fry; lightly pare the stalks and cut in ½-inch slices; top with ½ teaspoon marjoram for each 2 cups.

Cauliflower   Cut florets into 2-inch pieces; add ⅛ teaspoon celery seeds and 1 bay leaf broken into sections for each 2 cups of veggies.

Peas or pea pods (fresh or frozen and lightly defrosted) Add 1 tablespoon chives and ¼ teaspoon mint for each 1½ cups peas or pea pods.

Green beans   At this time of year, a package of frozen cut beans, lightly defrosted, is fine; top with ¼ teaspoon each oregano and rosemary.

Carrots   Shred 2 cups carrots and mix with ¾ teaspoon basil.

Asparagus   Wash, snap off tough parts of the stem, and cut in 3-inch sections; add ½ teaspoon tarragon for each 3 cups.

Salad Dressing for Spring Greens

ABOUT 1 CUP

Parmesan cheese, boned anchovies, macaroni, and tarragon vinegar all appealed to the "Sage of Monticello" who proclaimed: "I am an Epicurean." From his slaves, he learned the use of sesame, or benne, seeds; this recipe is adapted from one he served with the tender spring lettuce from his garden. Serve your salad with one of Jefferson's favorite dishes—macaroni and cheese.

1 clove garlic
$1/4$ teaspoon sugar
$1/2$ cup tarragon wine vinegar
2 tablespoons sesame seeds, crushed
2 tablespoons olive oil
2 tablespoons vegetable oil
$1/4$ cup water

Mash garlic and sugar together. Add all ingredients to a glass pint jar with a tight-fitting lid; shake hard. Allow to stand for 10 minutes and pour over fresh greens mixed with scallions as needed.

Growing Heirlooms

In Jefferson's time, vegetables were open-pollinated. You could collect the seeds from the current year's crop to grow the following year's plants. Many of today's popular varieties of vegetables are hybrids (you can't grow new plants from hybrids' seeds). They have been bred to be of uniform size, to ripen at the same time, and to survive shipping over long distances with less attention paid to taste.

If you'd like some old-fashioned flavor, experiment with heirloom vegetable varieties. For centuries farmers have collected the seeds from their best plants to save for planting the following spring. The best seeds were handed down from one generation to the next. These plants are open-pollinated, which means they reproduce seeds by natural processes. Cornell University offers a wonderful bulletin detailing sources of seeds and the history of many of the plants as well as cultural directions. To obtain a copy, send a check or money order for $3.40 to Distribution Center, 7 Research Park, Cornell University, Ithaca, NY 14850. Ask for bulletin 161-IB177. Start planning your Heirloom Vegetable Garden now.

ARBOR DAY
Last Friday in April

Apricots and Other Tree Fruits

Other Holidays repose upon the past,
Arbor Day proposes for the future.

—Julius Sterling Morton,
   Father of Arbor Day

The beauty and majesty of trees has long touched the spirit of humankind. In fact, one of the earliest forms of religion was the worship of trees. Gods "owned" the trees, and those trees were the homes of spirits. Mythology abounds with stories of gods and lovers being turned into trees. The river nymph Daphne, to escape Apollo, was turned into a bay tree. In Irish folklore, Baile "of the honeyed speech" died of grief at the falsely reported death of his beloved Ailinn, and an oak tree sprang from his grave. Ailinn, shattered at the news of Baile's death, collapsed and died; from her grave sprang an apple tree.

Apricots
Prunus armeniaca

Some Biblical scholars suggest that the fruit that caused such a stir in the Garden of Eden was the apricot (*Prunus armeniaca*). Now invested with the power of love, the apricot may also have been the mythical golden apple of the Hesperides that Earth gave Hera on her marriage to Zeus.

In the United States, Julius Morton Sterling, editor of the Nebraska *City News*, advocated improved agricultural practices and understood that the vast prairies needed trees to hold moisture and to serve as windbreaks. As a member of his state's agricultural committee, he proposed that an award be made to the individual and the county agricultural society who planted the most trees on the first Arbor Day, April 10, 1872. A million trees were planted. To this day, conservation groups, civic organizations, and schoolchildren in every state of the union except Alaska celebrate Arbor Day with tree-plantings and other conservation programs, often on the last Friday in April.

Almost a century after Morton's first successful Arbor Day, a new generation of Americans concerned about the environment chose April 22, 1970, to celebrate the first Earth Day. Tree planting was an important part of that and subsequent Earth Day celebrations, as more Americans recognize that care of the environment must be a daily responsibility of us all.

This spring, plant a tree in your yard or consider a tree at gift-giving times. Fruit trees make lovely gifts, and perhaps because they so graciously provide us with their bounty, they have been endowed with an especially gentle mythology—Eve's problems in the garden of Eden notwithstanding. The bounty of the orchard is truly a gift from heaven. For the bridal couple, the plum urges "keep your promises"; the peach invokes bridal hope; the apple "perpetual concord." Gift them not with a medlar, symbol of timidity and peevishness, nor the mulberry that speaks of unhappy love. The white mulberry, a cheerier choice, bespeaks wisdom and comfort, a nice Mother's Day gift. For a new baby, you might want to choose date palm, tree of life and abundance. The cherry offers hope of wealth and prosperity, and the hazel promises reconciliation and peace.

While your new tree grows, enjoy the fruits of someone else's tree.

Apricot Turkey

SERVES 10–12

½ cup brown rice vinegar

2 teaspoons molasses

2 tablespoons grated onion

4–6-pound turkey breast, cut in 1-inch cubes

1 tablespoon vegetable oil

2 cloves garlic, minced

1 cup white grape juice

½ cup water

1 tablespoon lemon juice

1 teaspoon freshly grated ginger

8 ounces dried apricots, slivered

2 tablespoons minced cilantro (fresh coriander)

Combine brown rice vinegar, molasses, and grated onion. Add turkey cubes and toss to coat turkey with marinade. Refrigerate for several hours or overnight. Drain turkey, reserving marinade. Add oil to heavy nonstick skillet, set on medium heat, and brown a few turkey cubes and the garlic at a time (if you crowd the pan, the meat will steam, not brown). Place browned turkey in a large casserole. Combine reserved marinade, white grape juice, water, lemon juice, and grated ginger; pour over turkey. Stir in apricot slivers and cover. Bake at 325° F for 30 minutes. Turkey should be tender. Stir in coriander. Serve over steamed rice.

———

Summer Fruit Soups

Buttermilk or yogurt blended with fruit and herbs makes a quick lunch or a fine finish to a summer meal. Combine ingredients, whirl in a blender, garnish, and serve.

Apricot/Geranium   For each serving, combine ½ cup fresh pitted apricots, ¼ cup apple juice, ½ cup buttermilk, ¼ teaspoon fresh lemon juice, and 1 small piece of rose geranium leaf. Garnish with borage flower and rose geranium leaf.

Orange/Fennel   For each serving, combine 1 cup orange juice, ¼ teaspoon minced fennel, and ½ cup yogurt. Garnish with grated orange peel and a sprig of fennel.

Pear/Ginger   For each serving, combine ½ cup fresh cored pears, ¼ teaspoon freshly grated ginger, 1 teaspoon lime juice, and ½ cup yogurt. Garnish with grated lime peel and Johnny-jump-ups.

Herbed Fruit

We seldom think about adding herbs to tree fruit. To flavor fruit dishes, we most often resort to the old reliables—cinnamon, nutmeg, and mace. Sometimes we try lemon with apples or almond extract with cherries. At Sage Cottage, we have found that herbs have the incredible ability to make fruit taste fruitier. Here are some herb combinations to try with tree fruits:

Apples: anise, bee balm, lovage, mint, poppy seed

Apricots: rose geranium

Avocados: chives, cilantro, cress, curry, dill

Figs: anise

Grapefruit: anise, mint

Lemons: garlic, onions

Limes: oregano

Oranges: anise, cilantro, dill, fennel, lavender, lovage, saffron

Peaches: basil, ginger, mint, savory, sweet cicely

WILLIAM SHAKESPEARE'S BIRTHDAY

April 26

Thyme

William Shakespeare, who was baptized on April 26, 1564, shared with his contemporary Elizabethan poets Drayton, Marlowe, and Southwell a grand sense of plants and nature, using them as metaphors for the human condition. Shakespeare carried his country background with him to the city, and his plays are replete with references to greenery.

Shakespeare likened the hair of one youth to "the auburn buds of marjoram." In perhaps the most often quoted herbal reference from *A Midsummer Night's Dream*, Oberon speaks of ". . . a bank where the wild thyme blows," that bower where Titania slept among the honeysuckle and roses. Imagine settling down for a nap wrapped in the sweet scent of thyme.

Pale lettuce-green, gold, silver, dark piney green; the many faces of thyme create a visual tapestry and a culinary smorgasbord. They are the backbone or, more

Thyme
Thymus vulgarus

appropriately, the "forebone" of the herb garden, filling in along the edges and under their lankier neighbors. Blossoms of rose, lavender, pink, and magenta appear magically atop fuzzy mounds or tiny bushes of thyme. One herb writer claimed that part of thyme's charm is the constant "traffic jam of bees and butterflies" that hover over the plants. Perhaps this is where thyme's reputation for activity (and courage) has come.

Whether there are, as Steven Foster has suggested, 400 species of thyme or 100 species of thyme with 400 names, in their infinite variety they create an ever-evolving pageant in the garden. The English garden writer Allen Patterson agrees that there are 400 species of thyme but separates them all into two classes: those that grow upright and those that blanket the ground. No garden ever has too many thyme plants. If you can keep several of them from blooming, you will have a steady supply of leaves for cooking until well after frost.

There is no argument that *Thymus vulgarus* is the most important thyme for culinary use. These tiny shrubs with pointed, dark green, ovate leaves are a bit more tender than the wild thymes, tending toward woodiness and winter kill but well worth the effort to maintain. This is the thyme of French cuisine.

No garden should be without some variety of lemon thyme (*Thymus citriodorus*). The lemony scent adds a haunting note to a beef stew, makes a lovely tea, and is both hardy and manageable. Low-growing caraway thyme, *Thymus herba-barona*, does indeed taste like caraway and perfumes a beef roast in a most subtle way.

Thymus vulgarus is a mainstay of New England clam chowder, glorious in creamed onions and green beans and useful in poultry stuffing, meat loaf, or with salmon and chicken. It enhances the flavor of potatoes, tomato juice, carrots, celery, cottage cheese, and mushrooms as well as zucchini and winter squash.

While a strong herb in its own right, thyme blends beautifully with many other herbs. In *Minnie Muenscher's Herb Cookbook* (Cornell University Press, 1978), the author proposed a wonderful combination of herbs that included one part each of marjoram, oregano, and summer savory to two parts of thyme that she dubbed "MOTTS." I double the savory, so my mixture is a more sibilant "MOTTSS," and I use it in any recipe that calls for marjoram, oregano, thyme, or savory. For an entirely different taste, substitute two and one-half parts lemon thyme for the garden thyme. Pick the herbs before they bloom and hang them in a dark, airy place to dry. When drying is completed, remove leaves from stems and combine in the proportions suggested. Store in covered containers in a cool, dry place; the larger the herb pieces, the better. Crumble them when you add them to recipes.

Thyme-Carrot Pasta

SERVES 4

This pasta dish is perfect for spring's unpredictable weather. You can quickly concoct it after a day joyously spent in the garden.

 1 tablespoon red wine vinegar
 2 large cloves garlic
 1 1-pound package frozen cheese ravioli (or 3 cups uncooked rotelli)
 1 tablespoon olive oil
 2 cups shredded carrots
 3/4 teaspoon dried thyme (or 2 teaspoons minced fresh)
 freshly grated cheese (Romano or Parmesan)

Put water on to boil, adding the vinegar and 1 clove garlic; cook the pasta according to package directions.

Mince remaining clove of garlic. Add olive oil to small frying pan; when slightly heated, add garlic and cook over medium heat for 1 minute. Stir in shredded carrots and thyme and toss until coated with oil. Reduce heat to very low, add 2 tablespoons of water, and cover. Drain pasta, shake over heat to remove excess water, and toss with carrot mixture. Serve with freshly grated Romano or Parmesan cheese.

_____

Thyme for Beans Dressing
¾ CUP

Thyme, characterized by Sylvia Wendle Humphrey as an "herb of fault-less charm" and whose scent Kipling compared to "the perfume of the dawn of paradise," combines authoritatively with the hot, rough flavor of garlic to redefine the taste of green beans. This dressing, sharpened further by the taste of yogurt, is wonderful on hot or cold beans or in your favorite three-bean salad.

2 tablespoons chopped fresh thyme (or ½ teaspoon dried)
1 tablespoon olive oil
1 tablespoon lemon juice
1 large clove garlic, crushed or minced
½ cup plain, low-fat yogurt
2 sprigs summer savory, minced (or ¼ teaspoon dried)
1 pinch freshly ground pepper
parsley or marjoram blossoms for garnish (optional)

Blend or beat together all ingredients and stir into warm, cooked green beans to be served hot or cold. Garnish with parsley and marjoram blossoms.

Silver Mousse

SERVES 6

Thyme in dessert? Try this—you'll delight in the light fresh taste. For a different taste, substitute lemon thyme. Our original version of this recipe was published some years ago by Bon Appetit in a small article about Sage Cottage.

> 1 tablespoon unflavored gelatin
> 1/4 cup cold water
> 1 1/2 cups white grape juice
> 1/4 cup sugar
> 3/4 teaspoon vanilla
> 2 large sprigs fresh thyme (or 1/2 teaspoon dried)
> 1 cup plain, low-fat yogurt
> red grapes and silver thyme for garnish

Sprinkle gelatin over water in medium bowl; let stand 10 minutes. Bring grape juice to simmer in a medium pan; add sugar and thyme. Stir until sugar dissolves. Remove from heat, strain, and add vanilla.

Beat hot juice into gelatin mixture; continue beating until gelatin is dissolved. Refrigerate until mixture just begins to thicken, up to 1 hour.

Beat gelatin mixture until frothy; fold in yogurt. Rinse a 4-cup mold with cold water and shake dry. Pour mixture into mold, cover, and refrigerate overnight. To unmold, wrap bottom of mold in a hot towel and invert onto a platter. Garnish with grapes and thyme. Serve chilled.

Thymely Growing Tips

Give thymes sun, a well-drained soil, and a little winter mulch (at Sage Cottage, we use cut-up Christmas tree branches) to prevent the shallow roots from heaving out of the ground with alternate thawing and freezing, and they will reward you with abundant crops for the kitchen as well as with cuttings to dry for fragrant winter arrangements and wreaths. Should you really be into quantity herb production, it's said that 6 pounds of seed will sow an acre of land and produce half a ton of the dried herb. Just imagine the heavenly honey that crop would produce! Last year at Sage Cottage, some scarlet pimpernel self-seeded among the caraway thyme and sage, creating a glorious combination of color, height, and shape.

MAY

After the uncertainties of April, no month is more warmly welcomed than May. Chaucer spoke for all of us when he wrote in "The Knight's Tale," "May, with all thy floure's and thy greene, welcome be thou, faire, fresshe May." May Poles, May Wine, and May baskets signify the hope and joy of spring and sound the clarion call for the new growing season.

May weather is often uncooperative and it can be a challenge to collect enough flowers for May baskets; still, a search of the garden and fields is worth the effort. Creeping out at dawn, on May Day, to secretly hang homemade baskets on the doors of neighbors' homes, generates an eminently satisfying feeling of being part of an ancient tradition.

This is the time to share the plants in your garden as well. Herbing is sharing. Pass along cuttings and root divisions to friends and neighbors. Fill a tub with sweet-smelling herbs as a gift to a school or a nursing home. Join the green spirits that herald the new season.

MAY DAY
May 1

Cicely and Woodruff

Garlands of flowers, couples carousing in the woods, bonfires on the hilltops, and dancing in the village square characterized May Day celebrations in England during the Middle Ages. Springing perhaps from ancient Druid rites, May Day was the year's merriest festival. On May Eve, young couples wandered through the woods, returning at daybreak, arms laden with flowers, to decorate their homes and the maypole erected in the center of the town.

Throughout Europe, May Eve was known as Walpurgis Night, a time for great bonfires to drive away the ghosts of winter. Beltane is the Celtic name for May Day. In Scotland, this ancient pastoral festival, when good folks are expected to be at home, is highlighted by Beltane fires glowing on the highest hilltops where the Druid gods were supposed to dwell. The evil winter, in the form of a straw effigy, was thrown into the flames to perish in a shower of sparks.

The dew of May morning, like the dew of Lady's-Mantle (*Alchemilla vulgaris*), was reputed to make one beautiful. In

Sweet Woodruff
Galium Odoratum

his diary recording his life from 1600 to 1669, Samuel Pepys explained that his wife was spending the night in Woolrich with friends "so to gather May dew tomorrow morning, which Mrs. Turner hath taught her is the only thing in the world to washe her face with."

Dainty, sweet woodruff (*Galium odoratum*), with its whorls of bright green leaves topped by drifts of white flowers, is the traditional centerpiece for May festivals. Symbol of humility, woodruff, known in France as *muguet des bois* (musk of the woods), has a scent likened to that of vanilla, new-mown hay, or perhaps fresh-cut alfalfa. Newly picked, the elusive scent doesn't exist, but as the sprigs wilt, the essential oil, courmarin, is released, and you are wrapped in a haunting fragrance. Once used as a strewing herb and still an ingredient in potpourri and snuff, woodruff is of great value as an air freshener. In early summer at Sage Cottage, we cut huge bunches and fill baskets with it for each guest room and all our bathrooms. A basket of cuttings will quickly rid a room of stale cigarette smoke or the lingering smoky odor that clings to clothes. Guests of Sage Cottage are always trying to identify the elusive scent that wafts throughout the house.

Sweet woodruff is most often recognized as an ingredient in May wine—a component no doubt encouraged by the ancients, who thought that sweet woodruff had the ability to make folks merry. This drinkable, fragrant herb has an additional endearing trait—it thrives in the shade and creates a dense ground cover. In bloom, the woodruff bed looks as if it has been dusted with snowflakes.

Lacy sweet cicely (*Myrrhis odorata*), a natural sweetener, is another denizen of the shade (although it prospers in the sun as well) that also appears in May. Its licoricelike flavor is particularly suited to the acid taste of rhubarb.

Tart and refreshing, tasting like no other fruit or vegetable, rhubarb was called "pie plant" by the early American colonists. The great mounds of huge, crinkly, green rhubarb leaves atop red stems create islands adrift in a sea of brown spring earth. If afforded full sun and a big helping of well-rotted cow manure after the picking season is over, rhubarb will flourish in one spot for years.

Since rhubarb is often beyond its prime when strawberry season rolls around, it makes sense to cut up 6 or 8 cups to freeze. When the strawberries are ready, you can make that ambrosia for salt-rising toast: strawberry-rhubarb jam.

—

Family Maibowle

SERVES 8–10

10 6-inch sprigs sweet woodruff
2 quarts white grape juice
sweet woodruff and violet flowers and leaves for garnish

Pick woodruff and allow it to wilt slightly; add 5 sprigs to each bottle of grape juice and refrigerate at least overnight but no longer than two weeks.

Using woodruff and violet flowers and leaves, make an ice ring to fit your prettiest punch bowl. Strain steeped juice and discard woodruff sprigs. Pour chilled juice over your elegant ice ring. Serve with a few tiny oatmeal cookies and drink a festive toast. A few sips and you'll agree with Chaucer that "Hard is the Heart that loves naught May."

Rhubarb Pudding

SERVES 6

This recipe for rhubarb pudding owes its inspiration to a recipe for Rhubarb Yorkshire from the Hancock Shaker Village. Because few of us are as hard workers or as hearty eaters as were the Shakers, this pudding, made with less fat and sugar, is 150 calories lighter per serving than the original. Thanks to sweet cicely, however, it is no less tasty.

2 cups rhubarb
1 cup finely minced sweet cicely (or ½ cup sugar mixed with
    ⅛ teaspoon crushed anise seeds)
1 tablespoon butter
1 tablespoon corn oil
4 egg whites
¾ cup flour
¾ cup skim milk
½ cup raisins (optional)

Topping

2 tablespoons butter
2 tablespoons brown sugar

Cut rhubarb into 1-inch lengths and cover with boiling water; drain and stir in sweet cicely. Heat 1 tablespoon butter and corn oil in a deep, 1-quart baking dish in a preheated 425° F oven; the fats should bubble but not brown.

Beat egg whites lightly; beat in flour and milk. Pour mixture into hot dish; sprinkle rhubarb/sweet cicely mixture over the top, keeping it 1 inch from the edge of the pan.

Return to oven; bake at 425° F for 20 minutes or until top is brown. Melt 2 tablespoons butter in small nonstick saucepan; stir in 2 tablespoons brown sugar. Cook until syrupy; drizzle over the top of the pudding. Serve topped with ice milk.

——

Stewed Rhubarb

4 CUPS

4 cups sliced rhubarb
¼ cup sugar
½ cup minced sweet cicely
¼ teaspoon ground cloves (or grated orange rind)

Pour boiling water over rhubarb. Allow to stand 3 minutes; then drain. Combine ingredients in a saucepan. Almost cover with water and simmer for 20 minutes. Enjoy on homemade granola or topped with vanilla yogurt.

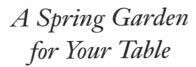

A Spring Garden for Your Table

Bring spring into the house. If you have lots of wild violets and sweet woodruff in your yard, dig up several small clumps that have flower buds on them. Tuck the plants into a flat basket (lined with foil) with some moss and bring them indoors for a lovely, fragrant display of fresh flowers. Once inside, the plants come into bloom very quickly; when their blooms fade, replant them outside.

CINCO DE MAYO
May 5

Specialties from South-of-the-Border

Back and forth across the Puebla city square and up into the hills, the battle rages between the fez-topped Zoaves and the serape-clad natives. Mexican general Ignacio Zaragoya and his troops finally repulse the French forces on May 5, 1867. The defeat of the forces of Napoleon III at Puebla signals the start of the French invaders retreat from Mexico.

Each year in Puebla, near Mexico City, the folk play *Batalla de Cinco de Mayo* reenacts the Mexican victory before enthusiastic audiences. Partisan crowds cheer the mock battle. The whole town is a fiesta. Street vendors sell *refrescos*: pineapple or other fruit drinks flavored with cinnamon to go with toasted *pepitos* (pumpkin seeds). Corn tortillas, baked on comals (grills sometimes made from a piece of scrap metal), filled with beans or meat and topped with scorching hot chili peppers and fresh coriander serve as a snack or meal. *Chili rellenos* (stuffed

Achiote
Bixa orellana

Poblano chilies) dipped in batter are fried and served wrapped in tortillas to soak up the oozing goodness (and the cooking fat). Sweet treats and spicy nibbles are available on every street corner.

It's important to remember that Mexican cooking is not all tortillas and chilies. Fresh local ingredients and ancient Mayan traditions meld with the cooking remnants of the invading French and Spanish to create a glorious feast of flavors. The cuisines of Mexico are as varied as the climates that inspire them. Subtly flavored moles, delicate flans, tender *nopales* (cactus), piquant *tomatillos* (green tomatoes), and pushy coriander join an overwhelming array of exotic fruits like papaya, guavas, and custard apples to create culinary delights that are both elegant and earthy.

The ingredients that once were limited to the Southwest are now available in supermarkets throughout the United States. Mexican green tomatoes are sold in cans as *tomates verdes* and fresh as *tomatillos*. This small, green, husk-wrapped vegetable is the basis for many salsas, gazpachos, and guacamole. The zesty flavor is most apparent when eaten raw. They add a mellow lemony flavor to cooked dishes. Tomatillos (*Physalis ixocarpa*) are related to the cape gooseberry (*P. peruviana*) and the North American ground cherry (*P. pubescens*) as well as to the inedible Chinese lantern; they are not related to the garden variety tomato (*Lycopersicum esculentum*).

Crunchy, crisp jicama (a member of the morning glory family) dipped in lime juice is sold as a snack. This tuber is used in the tropics in much the same way we use potatoes; or it can be sliced raw into salads or added to stir-fries, replacing water chestnuts.

Spices that seldom reach our northern markets lend an exotic air to Mexican cooking. *Epazote* (*Chenopodium ambrosides*) adds a slightly rank taste to black beans. The name comes from the Nahuatl words *epatl tozil*, meaning an "animal with a rank odor." (Note that some sources advise caution with the use of certain varieties of this herb, especially *anthelminticum*.) At Sage Cottage, we use bee balm (*Monarda didyma*) in its stead; the flavor is less off-putting to our north-of-the border palates.

Achiote, or annatto, is one of the most intriguing spices used in Mexican cooking, especially in the Yucatán. The small red seeds, looking like crushed brick, come from the *Bixa orellana* tree and are useful for both flavor and color. You'll find annatto listed as coloring agent on cheese and margarine labels as well as on lipsticks and soap. Having the consistency of gravel, the seeds require a ten-minute soak in boiling water before being crushed for use. In the Yucatán and some Cuban markets, you can buy it already crushed or made into a paste.

Mexican cooks often dry-toast herbs before adding them to dishes. This adds a more fulsome flavor to the finished product and seems to lock in taste, especially in long-cooking dishes.

———

Pollo Pibil

SERVES 6–8

To celebrate Cinco de Mayo, Poblano cooks spend days in the kitchen preparing one of Mexico's most festive and complicated dishes, Mole de guajolote (Turkey in Chili Sauce). Instead, we suggest you serve your guests Pollo Pibil (chicken cooked in a pit barbecue) from the Yucatán. The original recipe calls for wrapping the chicken in banana leaves. Since they are in short supply hereabouts, we discovered that a fine version can be prepared in a Schlemmer-Topf (German Claybaker). Another option is to wrap the chicken in brown paper and cook on a rack in an oven-safe kettle over boiling water (see recipe preparation instructions).

Seasoning Paste

1 tablespoon achiote seeds, softened in $1/4$ cup boiling water for
    10 minutes
*zest from $1/8$ of a grapefruit
*zest from $1/2$ a lime
$1/4$ cup grapefruit juice
$1/4$ cup orange juice
$1/4$ cup lime juice
$1/2$ teaspoon ground cumin
$3/4$ teaspoon dried oregano
12 peppercorns
4 whole allspice berries
6 cloves garlic, peeled
4 tablespoons white vinegar

*The easiest way to remove the zest is with a potato peeler; take care
  to get as little of the white membrane as possible with the peel.

Pollo

1 4-pound frying chicken, cut in parts with skin removed
1 large onion, coarsely chopped ($1 1/2$ cups)
1 16-ounce can peeled plum tomatoes, drained and cut in chunks
  (use the liquid for Cumin Baked Rice, page 139)

Combine all ingredients for the seasoning paste in a blender or food processor, process until smooth. Place chicken parts in a deep bowl and cover with seasoning paste, turning carefully to make sure that all parts of the chicken are thoroughly coated. Cover bowl and allow to marinate overnight in the refrigerator.

Soak *Schlemmer-Topf* in cold water; add chicken and all of paste. Sprinkle with chopped onion and tomato. Cover and bake in a 425° F oven for 1½ hours.

If you don't have a *Schlemmer-Topf*, rub a medium-sized brown paper bag with corn oil. Cover the top of the marinated and drained chicken with the seasoning paste. Lay tomato and onion slices on top, and slip the chicken into the bag. Fold the top of the bag over to seal. Place it on a rack in an oven-safe kettle. Add 1½ cups of water to the pan (it shouldn't touch the bag) and cover. Bake at 300° F for 2 hours.

─────

Mexican Salad

SERVES 4–6

Arrange match-stick size pieces of jicama, sliced tomatillos, and a sliver or two of fresh pineapple on a bed of lettuce. Pour Lime Vinaigrette over all. Sprinkle with 1 tablespoon minced fresh coriander.

Lime Vinaigrette

⅓ cup extra-virgin olive oil
¼ cup lime juice
3 tablespoons water
1 tablespoon Dijon-style mustard
freshly ground pepper to taste

Combine ingredients in a covered container. Shake to blend well.

Cumin Baked Rice

SERVES 6

1 tablespoon light olive oil

2 cloves garlic

¼ cup minced onion

⅛ teaspoon ground cumin

1½ cups long-grain rice

3 cups boiling liquid (Use tomato juice or juice from the tomatoes
    in Pollo Pibil [page 136] and water to make 3 cups or use stock.)

2 tablespoons raisins

1 tablespoon pepitas or pumpkin seeds

Add olive oil to a 2-quart ovenproof casserole. Sauté garlic, onion, and cumin for 1 minute. Stir in rice. Add boiling liquid. Cover and bake with the chicken for the last 15 minutes, or bake at 375° F for 18–20 minutes by itself. Toss with raisins and seeds.

Top your meal off with *guayabate* (guava paste) served with light cream cheese and crisp crackers. It's available in can or loaves in markets carrying Mexican or Cuban food.

Growing Tomatillos

Even though you can buy tomatillos in the grocery store, it's fun to grow your own. *Physalis ixocarpa*, the Mexican ground cherry, is a tender annual easily propagated from seeds. Sow in the early spring in a cool, sunny window in sandy soil. When all danger of frost has passed, plant outside, 1 foot apart in an open, sunny location. The fruit grows inside an inflated calyx or "bladder." If you live in a mild location, you may be able to overwinter the plants and increase your stock by dividing the roots in the early spring. The fruit is picked while still green.

THE FEAST DAY OF
SAN YSIDRO
May 15

Sesame and Other Seeds

Throughout New Mexico one sees roughly carved wooden statues of a farmer who walks behind an oxen-drawn plow, guarded by angels who hover at his shoulder. This is San Ysidro (St. Isadore, the husbandman), patron saint of farmers. San Ysidro was a devout man who sometimes spent so much time at his prayers that he neglected the tiny plot of land he tended for his landlord. A nosy neighbor reported the neglect to the landlord who, arriving to check on his property, discovered the field well plowed and tended. God, pleased with Ysidro's devotion, had sent two angels to plow the field. Melons, corn, wheat? There's no way of knowing what seeds San Ysidro was getting ready to plant, but since that time farmers pray to this plowman saint that their seeds will sprout and grow, that there will be rain for the crops, and that they will be protected from disease and destruction.

Sesame
Sesamun indicum

Agricultural peoples have always revered the power of seeds. Seeds are magic. They contain the life for next winter's food and the promise of next year's crops. They shelter the germ of life. Dorcas Brigham, in *The Herbalist* (the annual publication of the Herb Society of America), called seeds "packages of condensed life." They provide nutritious food and add flavor to that food. Sesame, ajowan, anise, caraway, cardamom, coriander, cumin, dill, fennel, nigella, celery, mustard, papaya—the roster of seeds for the kitchen is endless.

Of them all, sesame (*Sesamum indicum*) appears in more guises (and countries) than all the others combined. An ancient food (it is neither a spice nor an herb), sesame has been cultivated for many thousands of years. The flat seeds contain 50 percent oil, so sesame is one of the world's most important seed oils, and since sesame oil doesn't go rancid in the heat, it is especially suited for use in hot climates. Chinese sesame oil, made from toasted and pressed sesame seeds, produces a concentrated flavor much admired in oriental cooking.

The seeds, ground and mixed with the oil, create creamy *tahini*, used in Middle Eastern cooking. This runny paste flavors *hummus* and mixed with lemon and garlic, appears in salad dressings. Hummus—that calorific combination of garlic, chick peas, sesame seeds, and onions—can be served with fresh pita bread or as a dip for fresh vegetables. Crushed seeds with honey added becomes *halva*, a heavenly, nutty delight and a dieter's downfall.

From the Middle East, sesame seeds found their way south and soon found favor with the Africans. Called benne, sesame seeds reached the United States with those Africans who were brought here as slaves.

Caraway and fennel both self-sow wildly in the Sage Cottage garden. These seeds, crushed together in equal portions, complement each other in rye bread or any other dish where either is called for.

Seeds rescue salads from tedium. Poppy or fennel seeds on fruit salads and celery seed or dill with cabbage give a lift to the dish. The flavor is improved if you toast the seeds lightly and then mash them gently before adding them to your recipe.

———

Chicken Sesame

SERVES 6

juice of 1 lemon plus water to make 1 cup
2 tablespoons brown rice vinegar (or balsamic vinegar)
$\frac{1}{4}$ teaspoon molasses
2 tablespoons grated onion
1 teaspoon minced fresh lemon thyme
1 teaspoon grated lemon rind
$\frac{1}{4}$ teaspoon freshly ground pepper
3 whole chicken breasts, skinned and cut in halves
$\frac{1}{4}$ cup flour
1 tablespoons corn oil
2 tablespoons mustard seeds
$\frac{1}{4}$ cup sesame seeds
2 teaspoons brown sugar
2 teaspoons grated lemon rind
$\frac{1}{3}$ cup vermouth

Combine first seven ingredients in a medium bowl. Mix thoroughly. Add chicken breasts, coating carefully with the marinade. Cover and refrigerate. Allow to marinate for several hours.

Drain chicken, pat dry, and discard marinade. Add flour to a paper bag and toss chicken pieces a few at a time in the flour.

Heat corn oil in a heavy nonstick skillet and sauté chicken pieces on both sides until they are lightly browned. Transfer chicken to a shallow ovenproof casserole. Wipe out skillet with a paper towel. Add mustard and sesame seeds to skillet and cover. Shake over medium flame until seeds are lightly browned. Combine seeds, brown sugar, and lemon rind. Sprinkle mixture over top of chicken. Pour the vermouth into casserole (but not over the seeds). Bake at 350° F for 25 minutes or until tender. Serve with Seedy Noodles with fennel, tomato paste, and raisins, and steamed broccoli.

———

Seedy Noodles

SERVES 4

Noodles mixed with flavorful seeds and nuts make a quick and easy main course for a meatless meal, especially when paired with a green salad or steamed vegetables.

> 1 8-ounce package noodles or pasta
> 3/4 cup plain, nonfat yogurt
> 1/2 teaspoon cornstarch

Prepare one of the seedy seasoning combinations below. Cook noodles according to package directions, drain, and pour into a heated casserole. Combine yogurt and cornstarch, add seasoning. Combine with noodles, toss, and serve.

Seasonings

1½ teaspoons crushed fennel seeds
2 tablespoons tomato paste
3 tablespoons raisins, soaked in 2 tablespoons hot water

or

¼ cup slivered almonds
2 tablespoon poppy seeds

Combine and toast in heavy skillet over medium flame.

or

1½ teaspooons crushed caraway seeds, toasted
1 teaspoon dried thyme

or

1 teaspoon crumbled sage
1 tablespoon onion seeds
1 teaspoon minced lovage

Saving Seeds

Harvest seeds on a dry day after the dew has evaporated, just when they're beginning to turn from green to light brown (except for dill seeds that are harvested while green). Place a paper bag over bunches of stems, tie loosely, and hang upside down to dry in a warm, dark place where there is constant air circulation. Attics and barns are ideal, basements and kitchens are not. Shake seeds loose from the stems inside the bag. Pour seeds into a strainer and shake lightly to remove any small particles of leaves and stems. Leave out on a cloth-covered screen for another week or ten days. Store in airtight containers away from the heat.

AMELIA BLOOMER'S BIRTHDAY

May 27

Edible Flowers

Poor Amelia Jenks Bloomer. Schoolteacher and editor of a respected news journal, this nineteenth-century leader in the women's suffrage movement has become a footnote to history, remembered chiefly because a cantankerous rival editor dubbed the shocking new woman's garment of the time "bloomers." In point of fact, bloomers, the apparel that so shocked masculine sensibilities, appeared on the upstate New York scene at the instigation of Libby Smith. Amelia Bloomer simply published the pattern for them in her newspaper, *The Lily*. The first of its kind published by a woman, the journal was "devoted to the interests of women" and espoused the causes of women's suffrage, temperance, and the repeal of unjust marriage laws. No contemporary reference mentions why *The Lily* was chosen as the name for the news journal, but it's not

Nasturtium
Tropaelum majus

surprising when one realizes that Amelia Bloomer and most other women of the Victorian age were fluent in the language of flowers. The journal's name seems an excellent choice from a "flower speak" point of view. The lily symbolized sincerity and majesty and was thought to be a good-luck gift to women.

Today's magazines and menus are abloom with flower food. Sulfur-yellow daylilies and sweet pansy faces grace fruit plates. Blue-starred borage, peppery nasturtiums, and the pale lavender bells of chive blossoms decorate the tops of salads. Fulsome descriptions of this "new" trend of incredible edibles give little credit to the ancient tradition of flower food. When your garden begins to blossom, think of Amelia Bloomer and enjoy the flowers.

Before you start adding flowers to your food, a word of caution: Do not eat the flowers of plants newly purchased from a nursery—they may have been sprayed with an insecticide. Hose off plants before you plant them and then allow several weeks before you cut and bring them to the table. Better yet, grow your own plants from seeds.

As a general rule, the green parts of the flower are the least tasty. To avoid unwelcome visitors at the dining table, it's wise to check all the blooms for bugs. They hide in all the nooks and crannies. Add one tablespoon of vinegar to a cup of cold water, dip the flowers, and you will flush out most of the beasties.

Calendulas, nasturtiums, chive blossoms, and bee balm are among our favorites at Sage Cottage. They are easy to grow and will brighten your garden and your summer menus.

Calendulas, in India held sacred to the goddess Mahadevi, derive their name from *calends* or *calendar*, meaning "through the months." It's said that the Dutch used the dry petals in "hotch pots," or stews, adding the color but not the flavor of much more expensive saffron.

Nasturtium (*Tropaelum majus*), the other annual of our favorite foursome, is a triple-threat addition to the garden. The cut flowers lend a sweet peppery taste as well as bright color to breads; the soft green leaves and showy blossoms perk up summer salads; and the buds and seed heads (picked just after blooming) may be pickled and used like capers.

Standing like slender soldiers topped with lavender busbies, chives (*Allium schoenophrasum*) lend color and interest to the garden border in June. The delicate, bell-shaped chive blossoms inject a sweet, toasted onion flavor to breads and biscuits.

Bee balm (*Monarda didyma*), with its ragged, red flowers, brings a blazing presence to the July garden. A native of the northeast (with other varieties at home in other regions of the country), Monardas were used extensively by Native Americans. Bee balm leaves and flowers produce a fine summer tea. A few chopped bee balm leaves can replace *epazote* (*Chenopodium ambrosides*), especially in black bean recipes. The flowers lend an authoritative air to Hummingbird Bread (page 151).

Gold and Lavender Cups

SERVES 6

A quick and elegant spring appetizer, pungent, peppery nasturtiums, both flowers and leaves, have a memorable taste.

- 2 tablespoons minced nasturtium flowers
- 1 tablespoon chive blossoms, pulled from the stems
- 1 teaspoon poppy seeds
- ¾ cup low-fat cottage cheese

scant ⅛ teaspoon crushed lavender blossoms
18 dozen nasturtium blossoms, rinsed and debugged

Combine all ingredients, except nasturtium blossoms. Carefully stuff blossoms with cheese mixture. Arrange on a platter covered with nasturtium leaves and garnish with whole chive blossoms.

———

Hollyhock Lady Treats and Dragon Sandwiches

Little people delight in discovering wild food even if it is the cultivated hollyhock or snapdragon. Collect one open hollyhock blossom and one bud for each child. Invert the open blossom, pinch off the stem, and insert the bud stem into the top of the blossom. Poke a toothpick through the green on the blossom and your lady has arms. Use to top any fruit-salad plate.

"Snapping dragons" will make even the most pedestrian peanut-butter sandwich into something special. Collect several snapdragon blossoms and sprinkle over open-faced sandwiches. To make the dragon snap, pinch near the base, and the jaws will open—a sure giggle producer among the nursery set. Be sure to pick a few extras because tiny fingers are inclined to squoosh the flowers, shutting the dragon's mouth forever.

A word of caution: While these blossoms are edible, make sure you impress upon your tots that not all flowers can be eaten safely.

Hummingbird Bread

2 LOAVES

This bread combines a recipe for southwestern pueblo bread with bee balm, a native of the Northeast. The crust will be thick but tender. Wrapped and stored in the refrigerator, it improves with age.

1 package dry yeast
¼ cup warm water
2 tablespoons margarine or vegetable oil
½ teaspoon honey
4 cups flour
1 cup bee balm flowers (Use the soft red "petals" only; save the rough center part for dried arrangements.)
> ***or***
> 1 cup chive "bells" pulled from the blossoms
1 cup water at room temperature
1 egg white, lightly beaten

Dissolve yeast in warm water in mixing bowl. Add margarine or vegetable oil and honey; mix thoroughly. Add flour and flower petals alternately with water; beat after each addition. Knead the last of the flour/flowers mixture into the dough by hand.

Shape into ball and place in greased bowl, turning once to oil all surfaces. Cover with damp towel; allow to rise in a warm place until doubled in size (45 to 60 minutes).

Punch dough down; turn onto lightly floured board and knead for 5 minutes. Divide dough in half and shape into two round loaves. Place loaves 4 inches apart on a greased cookie sheet and cover with damp towel. Allow to rise for 30 minutes. Brush top with beaten egg white and spread more bee balm blossoms that have been dipped in the egg white over top of bread.

Bake in a preheated 400° F oven for 45–50 minutes or until loaves are lightly browned. While a bit too crumbly for sandwiches, this bread is wonderful toasted, brushed with a whisper of olive oil, and dusted with grated Parmesan cheese to accompany salads.

Flowers You Can Safely Eat

Common Name	Species
Bee Balm	*Monarda didyma, M. citriodora*
Borage	*Borago officinalis*
Calendula	*Calendula officinalis*
Chives	*Allium schoenoprasum*
Chrysanthemum	all species and cultivars except *C. cinerariifolium*
Dandelion	*Taraxacum officinale*
Daylily	*Hemerocallis*
Elderberry	*Sambucus canadensis*
English Daisy	*Bellis perennis*
Forget-Me-Not	*Myosotis sylvatica*
Hollyhock	*Alcea rosea*
Honeysuckle	*Lonicera* var.
Lavender	*Lavandula*
Mexican Marigold	*Tagetes lucida*
Mint	all species
Nasturtium	*Trapaeolum majus*
Pansy	*Viola*
Portulaca	*Portulaca grandiflora*
Rose	*Rosa*
Rosemary	*Rosmarinus officinalis*
Snapdragon	*Antirrhinum majus*
Violet	*Viola*
Yucca	*Yucca aloifolia*

JUNE

The etymology of the word *June* is uncertain. It could be named after Juno, the "Queen of Heaven" and principal goddess of the Romans, who blessed weddings and was the guardian of national finances. Some claim it comes from the Latin *jungera*—"to join"—from the union of the Sabines and Romans in this season; yet others declare that this month owes its name to *juniores*, for it was designated as the month of young men (May was reserved for old men).

While the etymologists disagree, the poets found a common beauty in this sixth month of the year. "The leafy month of June" does bust out all over like a red rose "newly sprung."

Summer is upon us. As you set about the season's work, remember Christopher Lloyd's cheerful advice from *The Adventurous Gardener*: "I have developed a capacity for not worrying when worrying will only take the pleasure out of gardening."

THE GREAT AMERICAN STRAWBERRY FESTIVAL

June

Red, Ripe Strawberries

A thousand years from now folklorists may write of the late twentieth-century spring ritual in which people of the northeastern United States combed straw-strewn fields on hands and knees, collecting tiny red fruits that were borne triumphantly to churches, firehouses, and parks. There the fruit was sliced, sugared, and served atop biscuits to throngs of worshipers who paid to sample the delicacy.

Strawberries
Fragaria

Come June, the Great American Strawberry Festival takes place throughout the land in celebration of my favorite June crop. Wild strawberries, called "heart root" by the Chippewas, were considered symbols of perfection and foresight. They have thrived in the United States since earliest times. Fields of them growing along the riverbanks of the Piscataqua in New Hampshire prompted Capt. John Smith to christen the area "Strawberry Banke" (now Portsmouth). John Winthrop noted on June 12, 1630, that his people had gone ashore at Cape Ann and "gathered a store of fine strawberries."

Today we don't think of this bright berry in medical terms, but in 1653 Nicholas Culpeper extolled strawberries as "singularly good for the healing of many ills." John Gerard suggested in his herbal (1633) that a decoction of strawberries "strengtheneth the gummes and fasteneth the teeth." These claims don't seem far-fetched when you realize that loosened teeth are a symptom of scurvy and that the delicate strawberry is a powerhouse of vitamin C.

The fictional Dr. Boteler, in Izaak Walton's *The Compleat Angler,* proclaimed that "Doubtless God could have made a better berry, but doubtless God never did," would have the support of generations of red-stained harvesters who know that there is no better way to eat these wondrous berries than fresh from a sun-warmed field.

For those berries you manage to save for desserts, a bit of anise flavor will enhance your recipes. Sweet cicely, at its best when strawberry season arrives, works perfectly for this. The strong anise flavor one tastes nibbling the leaves of sweet cicely melds gently with the fruit and enhances rather than overpowers the fruit's natural flavor.

The steam rising from a cup of the pale green tea made from the fresh sweet cicely leaves also carries the comforting aroma of licorice. These delicate, ferny leaves also add a fragrant and decorative touch to fruit salads.

In pre-Christian times, anise, another licoricelike herb, was perhaps used, along with mint and cumin, for the payment of taxes. Thought to avert the "evil eye," anise is one of the best herbal remedies for relieving gas in the digestive system, and as William Turner suggested in the sixteenth century, it "maketh the breth sweter."

Strawberry Shortcake

SERVES 12

The Rolls Royce of strawberry desserts is shortcake—a warm flaky biscuit, soaking up crimson strawberry juice and capped with a miniature mountain of strawberries and real whipped cream. If you're a weight watcher, savor a tiny portion of the real thing, then enjoy the rest of your berries sliced fresh. Don't settle for pretend toppings or sponge-cake bases.

$^2/_3$ cup milk

$^1/_3$ cup corn oil

1 cup all-purpose flour

1 cup whole wheat pastry flour

2 teaspoons double-acting baking powder

1 tablespoon sugar

$^1/_8$ teaspoon crushed anise seeds (or 2 tablespoons finely minced
   fresh sweet cicely)

2 quarts strawberries

$^1/_2$ cup cream, whipped, flavored with a little confectioners' sugar
   and $^1/_4$ teaspoon vanilla for garnish

Combine milk and oil in a 2-cup measure and chill in freezer compartment for 30 minutes.

In medium bowl, combine dry ingredients. Remove oil and milk from freezer, stir hard, and immediately stir into flour mixture just until ingredients are moistened and form into a ball. Divide evenly into 12 muffin cups that have been sprayed with vegetable spray. Bake at 450° F for 10 minutes or until lightly browned.

Serve hot from the oven, split in two with sliced and lightly sugared berries between the layers and on top. Garnish with just a touch of sweetened and vanilla-flavored whipped cream. Strawberry or sweet cicely leaves on the plate are a lovely touch.

———

Dutchman's-Breeches Sorbet

SERVES 6

If strawberries are the queen of spring fruits, in combination with a sweet white port they become the empress of desserts. Even if anise isn't your favorite flavor, don't leave it out. It enhances the flavor of the berries and wine without adding its own taste.

1 cup white port (tokay or black muscat), or any slightly sweet, robust wine
¼ cup sugar
¼ teaspoon anise seeds, crushed
1 quart fresh strawberries, washed and hulled

Combine wine, sugar, and anise in blender or food processor; whirl for 1 minute. With machine running, add strawberries, processing until they are liquefied. If your blender is small you may have to do it in two batches. Pour mixture into two ice-cream trays. Freeze until solid 1 inch from outside edge. Whirl the contents of one tray at a time in the blender or processor. Pour mixture back into trays, cover with plastic wrap, and return to freezer. Remove from freezer at least one hour before dinner and store in the refrigerator until ready to use. Serve with a glass of chilled white port and tiny vanilla-oatmeal cookies.

When the strawberry season is over, this recipe can be prepared with frozen berries (use two 10-ounce packages). Since most frozen strawberries are packaged with sugar, eliminate sugar from the recipe.

Strawberries and Then Some

Cover your prettiest glass plate with rinsed sweet cicely leaves and heap with lightly rinsed berries, hulls attached. Serve any of the following ways:

- With plain confectioners' sugar in which you've stored half a vanilla bean.

- Mix 1 cup plain low-fat yogurt, 2 tablespoons brown sugar, ½ teaspoon vanilla, and 1 tablespoon lemon juice. Use as a dip for berries or add sliced berries to the yogurt mixture and serve in sherbet glasses.

- For a fancy adults-only presentation, give everyone a wine glass of port, sauterne, or Rhine wine on a small plate with a small mound of confectioners' sugar. Dip the berries first in the wine and then in the sugar; finally, enjoy sipping the strawberry "wine" you've created.

Growing Anise and Sweet Cicely

Anise (*Pimpernella anisum*), an annual, should be sown in the early spring in rich, well-drained soil in a sunny location. The somewhat spindly, 1½-foot tall plants sprout quickly and should be thinned to 6 inches apart. In ten weeks or so, when the tips of the seeds turn slightly brown, they are ready to harvest. Pull the whole plant and lay on a screen to dry.

Sweet cicely (*Myrrhis odorata*) flourishes without full sun and enjoys a little extra moisture. Called giant chervil, this handsome plant with ferny, light-green leaves spreads by underground runners and is easily grown from seed (but the seed must be fresh!). Cut some of your plants back after they flower, and a new crop of lacy greenery will appear.

A BRIDE'S FEAST
June

Herbs for Fertility and Fidelity

A nosegay of bridal herbs beribboned and encircled with a scrap of antique lace is my gift to every bride whose family and friends stay at Sage Cottage. The centerpiece of our Bride's Garden is a collection of the traditional wedding herbs of myrtle, rosemary, and ivy (symbolizing variously, married bliss, remembrance, and undying affection) mingled with lavender, lemon balm, and a white rose. There's low-growing thyme, marjoram, and lemon verbena. Tucked here and there we've even included some herbs that were once esteemed as aphrodisiacs. The warm, rich, slightly anise-flavored fennel seed has long been used in love potions, especially around the Mediterranean. Southernwood, also called lad's love, was thought to be especially potent. We have been surprised to discover as we lead tours of the Sage Cottage garden that men, more frequently than women, find its scent more pleasing to the senses.

Caraway
Carum carvi

To our ancestors, many of the nuptial herbs were those thought to ensure fertility. The Jordan almonds tucked in tiny boxes by each guest's place are a relic of that tradition. To the French, almonds signified hope and fruitfulness. The waxy orange blossom finds favor at weddings because it can simultaneously flower and bear fruit, symbolizing the bride's ability to be both pure and fertile at the same time.

Prosperity and plenty for the newlyweds were often represented by grain. It was the custom for the grandmother of a Navaho bride to present the newly married couple with a special basket of cornmeal. Similarly, Roman custom required that a specially baked cake of salted meal be broken over the head of a new bride.

In all cultures and for many centuries, flowers and the fruits of the earth have played an important part in bridal traditions. The custom of flowers for the bride goes beyond her bouquet. The Breton bride's pink velvet apron is embroidered with roses, and the Magyar maiden's bridal chest is decorated with a red tulip, a symbol of passion.

German brides wore crowns woven with sprigs of the elegantly tidy evergreen myrtle (*Myrtis communis*)—sacred to Aphrodite and an emblem of marriage. It was believed that a sprig of myrtle over the door would keep love and peace inside.

Sage (*Salvia officinalis*) is thought to assure domestic tranquillity. Caraway (*Carum carvi*), the herb of retention, was thought to keep things from being stolen. Fed to pigeons to keep them from straying, it is supposed to do the same for husbands (provided the bride has the foresight to tuck a few of the seeds in his pocket on the day of the wedding). Cumin, a symbol of fidelity, is said to serve the same purpose.

A simple wedding feast from the Bride's Garden would be lovely for a small home wedding. Serve Love-ly Basil Orange Punch with delicate groom's cakes flavored with fennel and caraway; add tiny biscuits laced with rosemary and accompanied by a big bowl of fresh strawberry jam garnished with a sprig or two of lemon verbena. Cornmeal Sage Biscuits (page 272) with myrtle-flavored ham, garnished with sprigs of myrtle and lavender can make it a more substantial meal.

———

Love-ly Basil Orange Punch

SERVES 20 (6 OUNCES EACH)

You may choose to forego the Montenegrin custom of the groom and his father each presenting the bride's father with a plate containing a single sprig of basil, since this punch will allow you to share the basil with all the guests.

1½ quarts water
1 large handful fresh lemon balm
1 small handful basil (8–10 4-inch sprigs)
½ cup sugar
1 12-ounce can frozen orange juice concentrate
1 2-liter bottle ginger ale
orange slices and myrtle for ice ring
roses, violas, lavender blossoms, violets, or honeysuckle for garnish

Bring the water to a boil, add lightly crushed lemon balm and basil leaves, stir in sugar, cover, and steep 20 minutes. Defrost orange juice concentrate in a large pitcher, add 1 can water, then strain the herb/sugar mixture into the orange juice. Chill this and the unopened ginger ale until ready to serve. Make an ice ring in a large ring mold incorporating orange slices and a bit of myrtle. To serve, pour juice mixture and ginger ale over ice ring in a large punch bowl. At the last moment, float roses (red for passion and desire, red and white for unity) on top of the punch. Depending on the season add violas, lavender blossoms, violets, or honeysuckle. Surround the punch bowl with a ring of ivy, sage, and lady's-mantle.

———

Done-Roving Caraway-Fennel Crisps

100 SMALL COOKIES

5 teaspoons caraway seeds
5 teaspoons fennel seeds
5 tablespoons margarine, softened
3/4 cup sugar
2 egg whites
1 teaspoon vanilla
1/2 teaspoon grated orange rind
1/2 cup flour
1/4 teaspoon baking powder

In a heavy skillet over medium heat, toast seeds lightly; put aside to cool.

In a medium bowl, beat margarine until light, add sugar, and continue beating 1 minute. Add egg whites, vanilla, and orange rind, beat lightly. Combine flour and baking powder, add to bowl and stir in lightly with seeds.

On a lightly greased cookie sheet, place dough by half teaspoonfuls 2 inches apart. These cookies are thin and spread a lot; you might want to try test-baking one to get the hang of it. Bake for 6 to 8 minutes in a 350° F oven. Cookies are done when they are lightly browned. Remove from the oven. Allow pan to stand for 1 minute before removing cookies to a rack (if you use one of the two-layer cookie sheets, let them cool 2 minutes). I find it easier to turn the pancake turner over and use the backside of it to scoop them up. If they are too crisp and brittle to slip off the pan easily, pop them back in the oven for a minute. Allow pan to cool before you bake the next batch.

Store in an airtight tin.

Edible Bride's Herbs and Their Meanings

Almond: *hope, symbol of a happy marriage*

Apple: *perpetual concord*

Chrysanthemum: *long life, happiness*

Caraway: *retention*

Cinnamon: *dedicated to Venus*

Damask rose: *ambassador of love*

Fennel: *rejuvenation, longevity*

Forget-Me-Not: *faithful love*

Lavender: *constancy, loyalty, undying love*

Linden flowers: *conjugal love and marital virtues*

Love in a Mist (seeds only): *butterfly wings of our love*

Marjoram: *mascot flower for lovers (gypsy)*

Myrtle: *love, mirth, joy, emblem of marriage*

Orange: *happiness, prosperity*

Pansy: *remembrance*

Rosemary: *enduring love, devotion, loyalty, remembrance*

Sage: *domestic tranquillity*

Strawberry: *"you are delicious"*

Strawberry Leaves: *completeness, perfection*

Tarragon: *lasting interest, appeal, seduction*

ROSE FEST

June

Roses in Recipes

With fragrant petals tumbling over spiny stems clambering over walls and up trellises, the rose is the centerpiece of the June garden. Wandering about a garden of old roses, sweet scents wafting on every breeze, it's easy to understand why this blooming beauty played such an important part in the life of the ancients. More's the pity that many of today's roses are bred for appearance rather than scent, a fact that was a continuing cause for complaint by Katherine White when she wrote her gardening notes for *New Yorker* magazine.

Unlike the pushier scents of lilies and mignonettes, the fragrance of roses is mysterious and haunting. It's easy to believe, as did the Romans, that red roses are the flower of love, growing from the blood that Venus shed when she was wounded by Cupid's dart. A Roman symbol of success and valor, roses were also

Rose
Rosa

believed to be protection against drunkenness; they were strewn about the floors of banquet halls and fashioned into wreaths to crown the brows of revelers. Perhaps for this reason and because they were also used to crown the statues of Cupid, Venus, and Bacchus, roses were banned for use in the early Christian church.

In centuries past, roses were esteemed for their flavor and medicinal properties, as well as for their fragrance and beauty. Roses were an important part of the apothecary's garden, grown to be used in all manner of syrups and conserves to treat the ill and suffering. John Gerard lists twenty-eight "virtues" for roses, suggesting that they will cure "the paine of the eies," give strength to the liver and kidneys, and bring "comfort to a weak stomake." Red roses were most greatly esteemed for their medicinal qualities. If scent is equated with efficacy, one whiff of the apothecary's rose (*Rosa gallica officinalis*) will help you understand why. This rose, whose history we can trace back to 1300, is also useful for attar and fine potpourris. The achingly sweet, light crimson, semidouble flower is dusted with a golden, soldier's moss stamen—beauty and utility in one tidy package. Many of the old roses, especially the rugosas (rough leaved) and damasks, don't balk at the northeastern winters at Sage Cottage.

John Gerard allowed that "the distilled water of roses is good for strengthening the heart, & refreshing the spirits." He also suggests, "The same (rose water) being put in dishes, cakes, sauces, and many other pleasant things giveth a fine and delectable taste."

If you are fortunate enough to have some old roses, you can enjoy the "fine and delectable taste" of roses. Most old recipes start with "take a quart of rose petals,"—a bit much from a small garden. Should your garden be less prolific, more utilitarian, or nonexistent, you can buy rose water at most drugstores and some herb shops. Step back in time and use rosewater to perfume your life and flavor your food.

Rose Water

$3/4 - 7/8$ CUP

Gather the rose petals when the dew has dried but before midday. For all culinary uses of rose petals, snip out the nails (the white section at the base of each petal).

2 cups fresh rose petals
$1\frac{1}{2}$ cups distilled water
$\frac{1}{2}$ cup vodka
2 more cups fresh rose petals

To make your own rose water, place 2 cups rose petals in a glass container; add distilled water and vodka; cover and allow to steep in a sunny window for several weeks. Strain. Repeat, adding the remaining fresh rose petals. Strain and store in tightly covered jars or bottles in a cool dark place.

Add 2 tablespoons of rose water to your next batch of waffles or sugar cookies, or 1 or 2 teaspoons to fruit cup. A tablespoon in your favorite vanilla pudding recipe topped with rose petals (unsprayed ones, of course) creates a special dessert. It can also be added to inexpensive, unscented lotions to create the gentlest of fragrances.

Rose Vinegar

1¹⁄₃ CUPS

1 cup white wine vinegar
1 rounded cup rose petals

For delicate salads try a bit of rose vinegar. Add rose petals to vinegar in a jar. Cover tightly; allow to steep in the sun. Strain. Store covered in a glass container.

Rose Petal Salad

SERVES 6–8

1 quart washed greens (Ruby lettuce makes a nice contrast to the fruit.)
2 cups fragrant rose petals, with white "nail" removed
1 cup strawberries, halved
2 oranges, peeled, cut in sections, and drained
2 tablespoons rose vinegar (or 1¹⁄₂ tablespoons wine vinegar combined with ¹⁄₂ teaspoon rose water)
2 tablespoons corn oil
1 tablespoon minced sweet cicely
roses and violets or violas for garnish

Arrange lettuce on salad plate (a footed plate looks especially nice), sprinkle with 1 cup rose petals. Arrange strawberries in the center of the plate.

Place orange sections in a wheel around the strawberries. Beat rose vinegar, corn oil, and sweet cicely together and drizzle over all. Sprinkle with remaining rose petals and garnish with a whole rose or two and some violets or violas. Serve for a romantic bridal luncheon.

Growing Roses without Chemicals

During a visit to the show gardens of "Roses of Yesterday and Today" in Watsonville, California, we were advised to spray roses with a mild liquid-soap solution to get rid of aphids (the soap smothers the beasties). After spraying, allow to stand a few minutes; then hose off throughly to remove all traces of the soap.

We also plant garlic and chives around our roses. The artistic effect is grand, but the efficacy of the alliums as a bug repellent is still in question.

MIDSUMMER'S EVE
June 23

Herbs from the Good Spell Garden

On Midsummer's Eve—the Eve of Saint
John's Day—the sun seems to stand still
in the sky. Since pagan times, this phenomenon has been celebrated with bonfires,
revelry, and water play. The pre-Christian
sun worshipers built fires on Midsummer's
Eve, perhaps to symbolize their dependence
on the sun's life-giving rays or perhaps as an
offering to the sun asking for continued benefi-
cience for the new growing season. We can
assume at the very least that they were celebrating the return of warm weather and a season of
plenty.

Anise
Pimpinella anisum

    Midsummer's Eve is the night that witches,
spirits, and fairies walk the earth—a night of
magic. Herbs picked for medicine at midnight
or early in the morning before the dew dries
are deemed the most powerful of any harvested during the year. Fern seed
collected on the stroke of midnight will supposedly render one invisible.

    From earliest times, fire and smoke were thought to have mystical powers in effecting cures. On Midsummer's Eve in Europe, cattle were driven through coals and smoke to assure their well-being for the coming year. Coals from the bonfires were used to kindle new fires in homes to protect the inhabitants from harm for the next year. The ashes, a fine primitive fertilizer, were strewn over fields to assure bountiful crops.

As sun worship declined, the summer solstice became a time for lovers and romantic fantasy. Shakespeare based *A Midsummer Night's Dream* on this premise. Animals could speak, the fairies were abroad, and Puck assured one and all: "Jack shall have his Jill; Naught shall go ill."

From Puerto Rico to Switzerland, St. John's Day is a time for picnics and outdoor activities. Carrying provisions of ham, eggs and home-baked anise bread, villagers in Switzerland head up to the high pastures to celebrate with those who have been tending the goats since early spring. In Spain, name-day cakes in the shape of a *J* (for Juan) are baked for the occasion as are delicate rings of dough, fried in caldrons of hot oil and sold on every street corner. For reasons lost in history, Portuguese young men gift their chosen ones with pots of marjoram; the girls return the compliment with a bunch of leeks.

It's not clear why anise (*Pimpinella anisum*) is the chosen herb of the day. While delicate in appearance, this herb has a mighty licorice flavor. A most versatile herb, it is used in cakes and sweets, in Spanish soups and stews, and in Scandinavian applesauce. In thirteenth-century England during the reign of Edward I, the tax on anise paid for the repairs to London Bridge.

Pliny tells us that "this plant imparts a youthful look to the features and if suspended to the pillow, so as to be smelt by a person when asleep, it will surely prevent disagreeable dreams." Surely this is something to be wished for on Midsummer's Eve, as the dreams of that night are *sure* to come true.

For your Midsummer's Eve party, use some foods dear to the heart of revelers across the Atlantic Ocean. Since this is a night of magic and wonder, start your meal with a salad of greens from the "Good Spell Garden" (this is the spot at Sage Cottage where we grow plants that are supposed to make good things happen.) To create a simple but unusual menu, add steaming bowls of leek soup or leek pie, and anise cakes in the shape of *J*'s. Of course, you'll set the table with bunches of lady's-mantle and golden flowers, for Our Lady's plants protect us and yellow blossoms reflect the light of the sun, driving away the powers of darkness.

———

Anise Cookies

3 DOZEN

Low in fat and sugar and high in fiber, these cookies are a great nibble anytime. Your kids will enjoy helping form them into the shape of the letter of their own names.

> ³⁄₄ cup all-purpose flour
> ¹⁄₄ teaspoon baking powder
> ¹⁄₄ cup margarine, softened to room temperature
> 1 large egg (or 2 egg whites)
> ¹⁄₂ teaspoon crushed anise seeds
> 1 cup rolled oats

Combine flour and baking powder; blend in margarine until mixture is light; beat in egg and anise seeds. Stir in oats until well blended. Divide dough into eight sections. One at a time, roll each section into a $^{1}/_{2}$-inch round "snake." Cut into 2-inch sections and form into $\mathcal{J}$'s, or the letter of your choice, on a lightly greased cookie sheet (or drop by the level teaspoonful). Bake at 375° F for 8–10 minutes or until lightly browned. Store in a covered container or freeze.

———

Good Spell Salad

SERVES 4–6

Borage and thyme symbolize courage, sage offers the prospect of wisdom and long life, and marjoram speaks of joy. Fast-growing radishes—one of spring's first vegetables—if eaten on an empty stomach in the evening, it is said, will keep you from being bothered by a woman's chatter the following day. So this powerful combination offers courage, wisdom, joy, and peace.

1 quart young spinach leaves (or 1 quart young leaf lettuce)
$^{3}/_{4}$ cup radishes, sliced thin
$^{1}/_{4}$ cup thinly sliced, small, young borage leaves
1 tablespoon fresh thyme leaves, crushed
1 teaspoon thinly sliced fresh sage leaves
1 teaspoon sage blossoms (optional)
1 teaspoon minced fresh marjoram

Toss spinach and radishes with dressing. Add prepared herbs and toss again. Garnish with sprigs of fresh herbs.

Dressing
3 tablespoons mild olive oil
2 tablespoons red wine vinegar
2 tablespoons apple juice
1 teaspoon lemon juice
freshly ground pepper

Combine all ingredients and whisk thoroughly.

Other Good Foods from the Good Spell Garden

Angelica The best protection against evil, spells, and witchcraft, its name is derived from St. Michael, the archangel.

Almond An emblem of hope.

Bay "Neither witch nor devil, thunder nor lightning will hurt a man where a bay tree is."

Beans These will transform you into a king on Twelfth Night or, if spit in the face of evil spirits, will send them packing.

Calendula (Marigold) All the flowers named after the Virgin Mary were thought to be powerful against evil forces, enhanced in this case by the power of the yellow flowers to reflect the light of the sun.

Dill "Trefoil, Johnswort, Vervain, Dill / Hinder witches at their will."

Onions A sovereign protection against the plague.

JULY

Now comes July, and with his fervid noon,
Unsinews labor.

—The People's Dictionary and
Everyday Encyclopedia, 1883

July, originally called *Quintilis*, (the fifth month of the year in the old Roman calendar) was renamed to honor the birth date of Julius Caesar. It is a month filled with hot days, unexpected showers, and a bountiful harvest of herbs.

Has your garden become a chore? Are the weeds getting you down? Take heart—the Bible reminds us: "All the wide world of vegetation blooms and buds for you; the thorn and the thistle which the earth casts forth . . . are to you the kindliest of servants; no drying petal nor drooping tendril is so feeble as to have no help for you."

THE GLORIOUS FOURTH
July

Sunflowers for a Southwestern Picnic

Picnics are a glorious way to unwind. A picnic is for sitters and watchers, volleyball players and walkers—and especially for eaters. Picnics celebrate good food and offer the perfect opportunity to combine generations in an informal setting.

Within 10 miles of Sage Cottage, we can carry a picnic to the lakeshore, to a wooded spot overlooking a gorge, to the foot of a waterfall, or to our secret garden under the white mulberry tree. The food we enjoy can be as simple as a fast-food hamburger or a romantic spread featuring champagne and pâté. Picnics celebrate our oneness with the out-of-doors and are a joy at any season of the year.

Sunflower
Helianthus

What better picnic fare for an enchanted day than food from New Mexico, the land of enchantment, where all the days are cloudless and bright? The cuisine of northern New Mexico is a wonderful blend of Pueblo foods—corn, beans, sunflowers, and chili peppers—with those of the Spanish who began their march through the Southwest in 1540. Squash, gourds, and melons from Pueblo gardens fed the advancing Spanish troops. The squash blossom, the theme of so much Native American silverwork, was used in stews and soups as was sunflower meal. Watermelons, a favorite picnic food, described by Mark Twain as "Chief of this world's luxuries . . . when one has tasted it, he knows what the angels eat," were there, too.

The sunflower was found both cultivated and growing wild in the Southwest when the Europeans arrived. The experts suspect that it wasn't native to the region. The seeds were hulled, then pounded and rubbed on a metate or between stones to produce a rough meal that was made into nutritious and sustaining cakes. The sunflower was used in medicines and ceremonial rituals; the Hopis used it as a dye.

At Sage Cottage, we use toasted sunflower seeds, ground in the food processor or blender, as a delightful addition to meat and vegetable dishes, breads, biscuits, and cakes.

Pack cherry tomatoes and chilled melon along with bright handwoven napkins in your picnic basket, grab a blanket, and settle down by a waterfall, an ocean, or on your balcony with this distinctly American meal. You'll be all set to enjoy the best this world has to offer.

Sunflower-Squash Salad

SERVES 6

$\frac{1}{3}$ cup sunflower seeds

1 tablespoon corn or sunflower oil

3 tablespoons cider vinegar

1 large clove garlic, minced

freshly ground black pepper

$\frac{1}{2}$ medium red pepper, diced

2 small zucchini, cut in matchstick-sized pieces

2 small yellow summer squash, sliced in $\frac{1}{8}$-inch rounds

Toast sunflower seeds 15 minutes at 250° F. Whirl half the seeds in blender; add oil, vinegar, and garlic and a large grind of black pepper. Whirl whole mixture to blend. Put aside remaining seeds to use as garnish.

Arrange diced red pepper in the center of a high-sided platter, put zucchini matchsticks around the edge of the platter, and place yellow squash rounds between the two. Pour dressing over all and sprinkle with reserved sunflower seeds. Cover and refrigerate. The flavor seems to improve when the salad is refrigerated for an hour or so.

Skillet Bread

SERVES 6

3 tablespoons corn oil

1 teaspoon chili powder

1 clove garlic, minced

$\frac{3}{4}$ cup flour

$\frac{3}{4}$ cup blue cornmeal (or yellow, but the blue is sweeter)

2 teaspoons baking powder

3 tablespoons grated cheddar cheese

2 tablespoons coarsely chopped sunflower seeds

$\frac{1}{4}$ cup diced onions

$\frac{1}{4}$ cup diced sweet green pepper

$\frac{3}{4}$ cup milk

1 teaspoon honey

1 large egg

Add oil to 12-inch iron skillet over medium heat; add chili powder and garlic and heat together for 5 minutes. Remove from heat and cool.

Stir flour, cornmeal, baking powder, cheese, and sunflower seeds together in medium bowl; mix in onions and green pepper. Pour milk into large measuring cup; add honey, egg, and cooled corn oil/chili mixture; beat with a fork and add to dry ingredients. Stir until well blended. Pour mixture into the skillet that is still coated with oil. Bake in the skillet at 400° F for 25 minutes. Cut into wedges and serve immediately, or allow to cool, cut in wedges, wrap in foil, and freeze.

Stemming
the Zucchini Flood

Zucchini, zucchini—this gardener's nightmare can turn into pleasant dreams if you judiciously harvest some of the flowers (as well as those of any other summer squash) for salads, fritters, and stews. The blossoms with the little bump just behind the flower head will produce an endless supply of the ubiquitous green vegetable; collect some of them for cooking and you reduce the crop. Some people maintain that the larger male blossoms (without the bump) are tastier, but whichever you choose, they should be picked just as they are about to open. Watch out for bees when you pick closed blossoms.

BASTILLE DAY
July 14

Tarragon

On July 14, 1789, thirteen years and ten days after the American Independence Day, the French stormed the hated Bastille, initiating the events that would eventually free them from the rule of the Bourbon kings. Americans, who had not forgotten the support of the French in our struggle for freedom, were overjoyed at the news. The following year, Bastille Day celebrations were held to commemorate the great day, and in areas of the United States where French emigrés settled, the day was and continues to be observed with Gallic exuberance.

To celebrate Bastille Day as we do at Sage Cottage, give it a French flavor with the herb most representative of French *joie de vivre*—tarragon.

Recovered now from its battle with winter, July tarragon is lush and fragrant. The name, from the Latin *dracunculus* or "little dragon," may have been chosen because of its twisted serpentine roots or its sharp taste that bites the tongue like the fiery tongue of a dragon. *Artemisia dracunculus* var. *sativa*,

Tarragon
Artemisia dracunculus

cousin to mugwort and wormwood and beloved of French cooks, starts to flourish in July.

Pliny thought that tarragon staved off fatigue. Even into the Middle Ages travelers would tuck a sprig of one of the artemisias, especially mugwort, into their shoes before starting on a long journey. Seventeenth-century diarist John Evelyn thought that tarragon was "highly cordial and friendly to the head, heart and liver" (*Acetaria*, 1699).

The warm, peppery taste of tarragon is a welcome addition to egg and fish dishes, tartar sauce, and tomato soup. Chicken, vegetables, and salads all benefit from a touch of the dragon.

Just as tarragon prefers a solitary spot in the garden, it too prefers to be the star of its own recipes. Combined with parsley, chervil, and chives, it enhances flavor. Exercise caution, however—used too generously, tarragon wars with strong herbs like rosemary and thyme.

To preserve the taste for winter, pick large stems, rinse and shake dry, and pack in plastic bags for the freezer. The frozen tarragon won't do for salads but will add a lovely taste to cooked dishes. Or resort to that easiest of all tarragon savers, vinegar. Fill a glass jar with stems and leaves of tarragon, add half a lemon, then fill the jar with body-temperature rice vinegar or white wine vinegar (a drop on your wrist will feel neither hot nor cold). Cover tightly with plastic wrap and place in a sunny window for two weeks, stirring occasionally. Remove the lemon and tarragon, strain into sterilized bottles, add a fresh sprig of tarragon for "pretty," and cap with a nonmetallic lid. A spoonful or two will brighten the taste of potatoes, peas, spinach, asparagus, and salads of all descriptions.

Orange-Tarragon Salad

SERVES 6

Writing in 1699, John Evelyn reminded us that tarragon is one of the "perfumery or spicy Furniture of our Sallets." How it does perfume this lively summer salad! The sweetness of the oranges combines perfectly with the pungent bite of tarragon. This salad has enough character to combine well with barbecued meats and other picnic fare.

Dressing

2 tablespoons minced chives
2 tablespoons tarragon vinegar
2 tablespoons mayonnaise
2 tablespoons corn oil
1 clove garlic, minced
freshly ground black pepper to taste

Combine all ingredients in bowl or blender and mix well. Refrigerate, covered.

Salad

2 oranges
1 12–14-ounce package fresh spinach (or 6 cups loose spinach), stemmed
½ half head lettuce or bunch of leaf lettuce
1 small cucumber
2 tablespoons coarsely chopped tarragon
borage blossoms for garnish

Remove rind and white from oranges; section and chop. Wash greens, pat dry, and tear into bite-sized pieces into a chilled bowl with oranges.

Add thinly sliced cucumber; toss with dressing. Sprinkle chopped tarragon over all and garnish with bright blue stars of borage.

———

Tomato-Tarragon Soup

SERVES 6

This soup is grand either hot or cold.

>   1 tablespoon corn oil
>   1 small onion, minced
>   1 clove garlic, minced
>   2 tablespoons minced lovage (or $1/2$ cup minced celery tops)
>   1 49-ounce can tomato juice (In the summer you can whirl up fresh
>   tomatoes in the blender to make $5^1/2$ cups.)
>   1 bay leaf
>   4 allspice berries
> $1/4$ cup orange juice
>   2 tablespoons minced fresh tarragon leaves
>   chive blossoms or minced fresh chives for garnish

Heat oil in a $1^1/2$-quart saucepan. Add onion, garlic, and lovage (or minced celery tops). Cook gently for 3 minutes. Add tomato juice, bay leaf, allspice, orange juice, and 1 tablespoon tarragon leaves. Simmer together for 25 minutes. Remove from heat; strain. Add remaining 1 tablespoon of fresh tarragon; simmer for 2 minutes. Serve hot or cold, topped with minced fresh chives or chive blossoms.

Serve with Tiny Pineapple Refrigerator Muffins (page 208) or as an appetizer with roast chicken. For a delightful summer lunch, serve this soup with tiny, sliced chicken and radish sprout sandwiches.

Growing Tarragon

The taste of fresh tarragon is so different from the dried that it is an especially important addition to your herb garden. A sunny spot, good drainage, no close neighbors, and winter protection will reward you with bushy, aromatic plants.

Since tasty French tarragon (*Artemisia dracunculus* var. *sativa*) doesn't set seed, the only way to get plants is from cuttings or root divisions. Any seeds you may find are Russian tarragon (*Artemisia dracunculus*), a rangy, tasteless weed. When I recall that the tarragon plant in our garden at Sage Cottage is a descendant of the very first plant and has come down cutting by cutting, root by root, I realize how closely linked we are to the ancients.

Tarragon will survive in the house if you pot it up and cut it back, then leave it outside to experience several weeks of freezing temperatures. Bring inside, water it, and place it in a sunny window. New young sprouts should develop.

JUST BECAUSE IT'S JULY
July

Basil

Summer may "cum in" officially on Midsummer Day, but on my personal calendar it isn't a red-letter day until the basil is lush and ready for wholesale harvesting. No taste more truly spells summer than warm, spicy basil proclaiming its Mediterranean origins with Latin verve. The basil patch, basking in the late July heat, finally produces great green bunches to perfume pasta and fresh tomatoes, to create pesto and lively basil-garlic vinegars. Pesto, that glorious combination of basil, olive oil, garlic, and possibly nuts, is my personal summer staff of life.

Symbolizing love in Italy and grief in Crete and looked upon by the early herbalists with both suspicion and enthusiasm, basil teams enthusiastically with fresh summer tomatoes. According to Audrey O'Connor and Mary Hirschfield's *The Herb Garden Companion*

Basil
Ocimum basilicum

(Cornell University Press, 1984), rhyme basil with dazzle when speaking about this most ambiguous of herbs and your pronunciation will be perfect.

While nothing compares to the taste of fresh basil, fresh leaves blended with water and frozen in ice-cube trays or a strong basil vinegar are welcome reminders of summer when the snow is banked around the door. A quart jar, filled with lightly crushed basil, topped to the brim with a good red wine vinegar, covered with a plastic lid, and allowed to sit in the sun for several weeks is a wonderful way to extend the season. Strain and bottle for winter use.

Half of our basil vinegar is always generously laced with garlic; two cloves to a pint seem about right. A tablespoon or two of this elixir will enhance the most pedestrian of soups and can replace salt in the cooking of pasta. Mixed with an equal part of olive oil or yogurt, either of these vinegars creates the simplest but tastiest of salad dressings.

For a new taste sensation, drizzle a mustardy vinaigrette over a platter of cantaloupe and sliced tomatoes and sprinkle a heaping teaspoon of minced basil over all.

Ritzy Sloppy Joes

SERVES 6

This is fine for both the family and company and is really best made with dried basil. Easy to make, it also freezes well. Serve on lightly toasted whole wheat hamburger rolls, over oven-cooked rice, or rolled in flour tortillas with shredded lettuce and tomatoes on top.

1 tablespoon corn oil
2 medium onions, coarsely chopped
1 tablespoon water
1½ pounds lean ground beef
1 6-ounce can tomato paste
2 teaspoons dried basil
3 tablespoons brown rice vinegar
1 tablespoon A.1. Steak Sauce
1 tablespoon Worcestershire sauce
¼ cup maple syrup
½ cup dry red wine (or 1½ tablespoons red wine vinegar,
   with water added to make ½ cup)

Add oil to Dutch oven over medium heat, add onions. Toss with oil, add 1 tablespoon water, and cook until limp. Add ground beef and cook until all the pink is gone. Add remaining ingredients; simmer for 25 minutes.

Basil Zucchini Pancakes

16 SMALL PANCAKES

1 cup all-purpose flour
1¾ teaspoons double-acting baking powder
¼ teaspoon baking soda
⅓ cup low-fat cottage cheese
1 egg white, lightly beaten
1 cup grated zucchini
2 tablespoons minced fresh basil
¾ to 1 cup white grape juice

Combine flour, baking powder, and baking soda in medium bowl. Combine cottage cheese, egg white, zucchini, and basil in a small bowl with half of the grape juice. Stir cottage cheese mixture into the dry mixture. Add remaining juice until you have a medium-thin batter about the consistency of heavy cream (the amount of juice will vary with the wetness of the zucchini).

Spread by rounded tablespoonfuls on a heated griddle that has been lightly greased. Cook until brown, turn, and cook on the other side. Serve with Tomato-Coriander-Orange Topping (recipe follows).

Tomato-Coriander-Orange Topping

APPROXIMATELY 3 CUPS

1⅓ cups peeled and cubed fresh tomatoes with juice discarded
    (or 1⅓ cups drained, cubed, canned plum tomatoes)
1 12-ounce can (undiluted) frozen apple juice concentrate
1½ teaspoons grated orange rind
¼ cup orange juice
1 tablespoon sugar
¼ teaspoon ground coriander seeds
1 teaspoon minced fresh coriander (cilantro)
2 teaspoons cornstarch combined with 2 tablespoons water

Combine first five ingredients in a medium saucepan. Cook over low heat, stirring frequently for 20 minutes. Add ground and minced corianders and water and cornstarch mixture. Cook, stirring carefully, an additional 5 minutes. Serve warm with zucchini pancakes or cold with low-fat yogurt.

Fresh Winter Basil

One morning over breakfast at Sage Cottage, one of our guests told us how she grew basil all winter on her windowsill . . . in Chicago . . . in an apartment. Knowing how much sun basil needs and how many failures I had experienced trying to bring seedlings into the house in the fall, I was skeptical. But after giving the effort another try last winter, I can report moderate success.

Use a small plastic planter box, 10x4x4 inches, with its own tray. Fill it with a sterile starting mix, sow the seed generously, sprinkle a little more potting mix on top and then soak the whole container in warm water until the soil is uniformly wet. Lay a piece of dampened newspaper over the planter and keep moist. Set the planter in a warm (but not sunny) place. Wait for seedlings to appear. As soon as a good portion of the seeds have germinated, remove the newspaper and place the planter in a sunny window. If you try this during November, December, January, February, and March, a little extra fluorescent light is helpful, as is a dilute solution of Peters Plant Food applied every other week.

Start snipping bits of basil as soon as the first set of true leaves appears. These first cuttings add a welcome bit of summer to winter salads. Keep snipping and using. Don't expect huge, robust plants—the seedlings will never grow more than 5 or 6 inches tall, nor will they develop the strong flavor of garden-grown basil—but they are still a delight. Start a second pot three or four weeks after the first one. When the second is ready to use, scrub out the first container and start over.

It's important to use fresh, sterile soil each time and to scrub the pot carefully between plantings. Various fungi are the most common disease causes in culinary herbs. The best way to prevent infection is to keep the foliage as dry as possible by watering early in the day and watering the *soil*, not the plant.

BEATRIX POTTER'S BIRTHDAY

July 28

Peter Rabbit's Favorites

First he ate some lettuces and some French beans; and then he ate some radishes.

—The Tale of Peter Rabbit

Few children's writers have invested their books with the skillful coordination of words and pictures as did Beatrix Potter. Without playmates to distract her, the young Beatrix focused her full attention on discovering and depicting the world around her. Born on July 28, 1866, this shy, lonely child was constantly at work with pencil and paper, creating portraits of her ever-expanding menagerie and collection of natural things. Growing things fascinated her. As she grew older, her pictures became more detailed and botanically correct while still retaining an artistic air.

Potter's efforts to create a life of her own were hampered by her Victorian

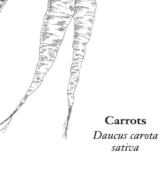

Carrots
Daucus carota sativa

English family who, according to the customs of the time, expected their unmarried daughter to remain at home at their beck and call.

Yet she persisted. The drawings that eventually illustrated her popular books were originally conceived to illustrate letters to the children of her former governess. With the publication of the colored edition of *The Tale of Peter Rabbit* in 1901, Potter began her escape into independence and eventually at thirty-eight, into a satisfying marriage and life as a farmer.

Potter's special blend of imagination and reality imbued her books with a timeless sense of place. Her gardens abounded with flowery heads of cabbage, tender orange carrots, and succulent lettuces. Pea vines rambled up twig trellises, and one can almost smell the onions Benjamin Bunny collected for his aunt. Even a little herbal doctoring found its way into the stories, for wasn't Peter dosed with chamomile tea after gorging himself in Mr. MacGregor's garden?

While generations of children have been delighted with the stories and the graceful depiction of garden produce, they are a good deal less enthusiastic about actually eating the stuff. Small fry, it seems to me, are much like the characters in a Beatrix Potter book; they are delighted with fresh, raw vegetables but very resistant to consuming them cooked. If you'd like to encourage your family to enjoy more of the green (and orange and red) goodies, season them with herbs and leave behind the butter and heavy sauces that disguise their flavor.

These vegetable recipes would please a small person I know who, when asked just what was the matter with the veggies on her plate, replied: "Yuck! They taste so green!"

Potatoes

Add a generous tablespoon of red wine vinegar to cooking water for potatoes.

Butter and sour cream seem to be the operative words when it comes to potatoes, but these simple variations make for more healthful eating.

- In a nonstick skillet, sauté ⅓ cup watercress in 1 teaspoon olive oil until limp. Toss with 1 pound boiled new potatoes (with the skins on); add 1 tablespoon minced chives and 2 tablespoons plain, low-fat yogurt and toss again. Serve hot. Serves 4.

- Toss 2 cups hot cooked cubed potatoes with 1 teaspoon Dijon-style mustard mixed with 1 tablespoon cottage cheese. Add 1 teaspoon minced fresh dill, 1 tablespoon minced fresh parsley, and 2 teaspoons minced fresh chives; toss again. Serves 4 as a side dish.

- Add 1 teaspoon minced fresh rosemary or ¾ teaspoon crushed fennel seeds and ¾ teaspoon crushed caraway seeds to your favorite scalloped potato recipe.

Spinach

- Thinly slice 1 clove garlic. Sauté in 1 teaspoon olive oil in nonstick skillet until soft. Add 1 10-ounce package washed fresh spinach (large stems removed), or 1 package frozen chopped spinach, defrosted. Cover, cook 3 minutes. Stir in 1 tablespoon minced fresh basil (or ¾ teaspoon dried) and 1 teaspoon minced fresh lemon verbena. Cover; cook 1 minute. Toss with 1 tablespoon garlic red wine vinegar. Serve garnished with calendula blossoms. Serves 4.

- Toss cooked spinach with $1/8$ teaspoon ground nutmeg and 1 tablespoon tarragon/garlic vinegar.

Red and Green Peppers

Core, remove seeds, and slice 1 red and 1 green pepper; thinly slice 1 large onion and 1 clove of garlic. In a nonstick skillet over medium heat, toast $1/2$ teaspoon crushed cumin seeds. Add $1/2$ teaspoon olive oil and vegetables. Toss to coat with oil and cumin. Add $1/2$ cup white grape juice. Cover and cook over low heat until peppers are soft and lightly glazed. Serve in halved, toasted pita-bread pockets, or toss with cooked pasta. Serves 2 if in pita pockets, 6 with pasta.

Red Cabbage

Add $3/4$ teaspoon crushed caraway seeds, and $1/4$ teaspoon crushed celery seeds to a nonstick skillet and toast lightly over medium heat. Add 4 cups shredded red cabbage to seeds in pan, stir in $1/2$ cup purple grape juice. Cover and cook over low heat until cabbage is tender, but not mushy. Serves 6.

Beets

Drain liquid from two 1-pound cans julienned beets, reserving one half the liquid (add the remainder to your collection of vegetable juice for stock). Add beet juice, 2 tablespoons red wine vinegar, 2 tablespoons frozen apple juice concentrate, and 1 teaspoon grated fresh ginger root to a medium sauce pan. Heat to boiling. Combine $1^1/2$ teaspoons cornstarch with 1 tablespoon water. Pour several tablespoons of the hot juice into the cornstarch mixture; then add to boiling liquid in pan. Cook until sauce is thickened. Add beets and heat through. Serves 6–8.

More Tasty Herbs for Vegetables

These combinations will add to your enjoyment of summer's bounty. Add 1 tablespoon minced fresh herbs or ¾ teaspoon dried herbs for each 2 cups of vegetables. Taste and add more if necessary.

Tarragon tickles asparagus,

Basil becomes tomatoes, carrots, and potatoes,

Thyme is a treat with carrots and squash,

Rosemary reanimates potatoes, peas, and spinach,

Mint melds with peas,

Dill is delightful with broccoli, corn, and beets.

AUGUST

August is roadsides draped in Queen Anne's lace and bejeweled with sky-blue chicory and bright goldenrod. The garden overflows with tomatoes and melons. It's time for the gardener to sit back, relax, and enjoy the fruits of the summer's labor.

Once called *Sextils*, August was renamed and lengthened to suit the vanity of Caesar Augustus and to commemorate his personal triumphs. He decreed that it should be equal in length and extent to July, which honored his predecessor, Julius.

Throughout the world, it is a time for harvest. This is a good time to add a few more calendulas to the dried flower collection, harvest oregano, and even collect a bit more lemon thyme, provided you kept it from blossoming.

This is the early afternoon of the year. The garden is marked, as Ernest Hemingway described preparations for a bullfight, by "A growing ecstasy of ordered, formal, passionate, increasing disregard for death."

LAMMAS DAY
August 1

Herbs in Breads

Since the time of the early Anglo-Saxons, August 1 has been celebrated as Lammas Day—a time to honor the new crop of wheat. The name came from the Old English *hlafmaes*, or "loaf mass," for this was the time when bread, baked from the first ripe grain of the new harvest, was presented at the church to be blessed.

Other civilizations celebrate their grain harvests with equal enthusiasm because of grain's importance as a survival food. It is, in truth, the staff of human life. The East lived on rice, Europe on wheat and oats, and the New World on maize. While Americans call maize "corn," Western Europe refers to any indigenous grain as corn.

Wheat
Triticum sativum

Grain, because of its essential role in human diet, has been invested with religious and mythical properties. Grain planting and grain harvesting are, in most cultures, attended with much ceremony. In many cultures, the last stalk of grain in the field is thought to contain the soul of the plant; it is carefully preserved to bring good luck and a good harvest the following year.

Breads, too, have fallen under the cloak of ritual. Loaves produced from the first harvesting, it is said, contain the spirit of the grain, a spirit to be indulged and worshiped. The flat bread of India and the Middle East, the rough rye and pumpernickel of northern European countries, and the delicate croissants at the French breakfast table tell us something about the people who bake and eat them. We know, for example, that as people have become more affluent, they eschew the dark breads of the countryside in favor of refined flour—to the detriment of their health.

No one who has ever tasted a loaf of bread fresh and warm from the oven could disagree with the old Spanish proverb: "All sorrows are less with bread."

Whatever form your bread takes, it is tastier with a variety of flours. Wheat adds gluten to make the bread rise, corn brings crunchiness and sweetness to the loaf, and rye adds its own malty body to the mixture. Oatmeal, oat bran, and rice bran also lend sweetness and texture.

Each year at Sage Cottage, we turn out loaves and loaves of herb breads for toast and thousands of tiny, herb-laced baking powder biscuits. At a bed-and-breakfast inn, breads are indeed the staff of life.

Sour Milk Herb Biscuits

30 BISCUITS

Producing a light, flaky biscuit without the use of solid shortening is a real challenge. These $1^1/_2$-inch morsels are tender and cakelike, a perfect foil for herb jams and jellies. At Sage Cottage, we don't create sweet breads for breakfast; we serve them plain so that each guest may add the degree of sweetness he or she chooses.

The secret of good biscuits is a light touch. Combine the wet and dry ingredients with a fork in as few strokes as possible. We use a $1^1/_2$-inch-round cutter that is also $1^1/_2$-inches high. Cut the biscuits straight down. Don't twist or you'll seal the edges and keep the biscuits from rising properly.

> 2 cups all-purpose flour (or see other combinations below)
> 2 teaspoons double-acting baking powder (or 3 teaspoons low-sodium baking powder)
> herbs (see below)
> $^1/_2$ teaspoon baking soda
> $^1/_3$ cup liquid vegetable oil
> 1 tablespoon lemon juice with enough skim milk added to make $^1/_2$ cup (or see other liquids below)

Combine flour(s), baking powder, herbs, and baking soda in a medium bowl. Add oil to milk mixture. Do not stir. Make a hole in the center of the dry ingredients and pour in liquid. Stir lightly with a fork until dough pulls away from the side of the bowl. Flours vary, so you may have to add more liquid. Turn the dough out onto a lightly floured board and roll it out to $^1/_2$-inch thickness. Cut as many biscuits out of the dough as possible and place them touching one another on an ungreased cookie sheet. Lightly reroll dough and cut more biscuits until all the dough is used up. Bake in a 450° F oven for 10 minutes or until lightly browned. Serve hot.

Liquid Substitutions Replace milk with an equal amount of the following:
- orange or pineapple juice (delete lemon juice)
- water plus the juice and grated rind of 1 lemon
- apple or grape juice plus 1 teaspoon vinegar

When using juice, reduce the oven temperature to 425° F to prevent burning.

Flour Replace ⅔ cup of the white flour with whole wheat, rye, buckwheat, or oat or rice bran.

Herbs Experiment; try out new tastes. This is an inexpensive way to test herb combinations. Try adding these:
- 2 tablespoons minced fresh chive or oregano blossoms
- 3 tablespoons minced fresh bee balm flowers
- ¼ teaspoon cinnamon, ¼ teaspoon grated lemon peel, and ¼ teaspoon ground cloves (especially good with apple juice)
- 1 tablespoon minced rose geranium leaves
- 2 tablespoons minced fresh basil (or 2 teaspoons dried); nice with orange juice
- ¾ teaspoon crushed fennel seeds and ½ teaspoon crushed caraway seeds (with some rye flour)
- ¼ cup minced fresh calendula petals with pineapple juice
- 1 teaspoon minced fresh mint with 2 teaspoons minced fresh parsley and 1 teaspoon minced chives (You can use ½ teaspoon dried mint, but don't use dried parsley.)

Refrigerator Muffins

5 DOZEN

Muffin mania seems to have swept the country. This recipe is a yummy, more healthful alternative to store-bought varieties. They are perfect for the cook who doesn't want to dirty the kitchen every morning to put hot muffins on the table. One mixing does it all—you simply add herbs or fruits, at your whim, when you bake them. The mixture will last for up to 4 weeks in the refrigerator.

1 12-ounce box bite-sized shredded wheat cereal
1 quart buttermilk
1 cup corn oil
8 egg whites, lightly beaten
2 cups whole wheat flour
1 cup oat flour (Whirl rolled oats in blender or food processor until it's coarse but not powdery, or use 1 cup fine cornmeal.)
1 cup all-purpose flour
5 teaspoons baking soda
²/₃ cup brown sugar

Pour shredded wheat into a very large bowl. Add buttermilk and allow to stand for 10 minutes. Stir in corn oil and egg whites. Combine flours, baking soda, and brown sugar in another bowl. Stir lightly into liquid mixture. Refrigerate overnight. Spray as many muffin cups as you want to use with vegetable oil. Add flavorings to individual muffin cups (see below). Fill muffin cups half full. Bake 18–20 minutes in a 400° F oven. Tightly covered, the mixture will last up to 2 weeks in the refrigerator.

Flavorings for Muffins

- Add 1 small sage leaf, verbena leaf, or tiny sprig of tarragon to bottom of each muffin cup. Add muffin mix. Poke 1 teaspoon white grape jelly into center of each muffin.
- Sprinkle each muffin cup with some cinnamon and ¼ teaspoon brown sugar. Add 1 teaspoon raisins or currants to each muffin.
- Poke a drained pineapple tidbit into each muffin. Sprinkle lightly with powdered ginger.

Instead of Wheat Flour

While gluten in wheat flour "holds the rise" in yeast breads, it is a real dietary problem for many people. You can buy gluten-free bread (usually in the frozen-food case of your local health food store) or you can adapt your recipes with other flours. These substitutions may make a heavier product, but they also add wonderful flavor.

1 cup wheat flour equals:

$3/4$ cup coarse cornmeal

1 cup fine cornmeal or corn flour

$7/8$ cup buckwheat flour

$1\frac{1}{8}$ cups rolled oats (whirled in the blender until fine)

$7/8$ cup barley flour

SAN LORENZO'S FEAST DAY
August 10

Tomatoes

If you are in northern New Mexico on August 10, head north on the River Road that leads from Santa Fe to Taos. Near Penasco turn left, and there, tucked away in a valley at the foot of the Sangre de Christo Mountains, stands Picuris Pueblo. This is the feast day of San Lorenzo, the saint for whom the first

Tomatoes
Lycopersicon escuentum var.

village church, built by Spanish missionaries in the sixteenth century, was named. In these parts San Lorenzo, usually shown carrying the grill on which he was martyred, is charged with the success of the August crops—no mean task in this arid, high mountain area where the frost often nips the corn crop.

To the rest of the world, St. Lawrence is patron saint of cooks and winemakers. How appropriate that the feast day of a saint charged with the well-being of cooks and August crops comes when tomatoes, those pillars of world cuisine, hang heavy and sweet on the vine.

The first tomatoes, tiny, ridged, and probably yellow, grew unappreciated in Peru or Ecuador. Archaeological evidence suggests that through centuries of deliberate selection, domestic crops of tomatoes, winter squash, beans, avocados, and corn were staples of the diet of Central Americans as far back as 3500 B.C. The Spaniards found *tomatl* (a Nahuatl or Aztec word) growing in Montezuma's garden in 1519.

After tomatoes arrived in Europe, in the early sixteenth century, two great debates began. Was this strange plant *pomo doro* (golden apple), or should it more properly be called *pomi dei Moro* (Moor's apple) or the romanticized French, *pomme d' amour* (love apple)? The amorously inclined must have prevailed, for by the time John Gerard wrote his herbal in 1633, he spoke of "Apples of Love." Thus *tomatl* became the "love apple" and was invested with the powers of an aphrodisiac. The other controversy centered on the edibility of this new plant that was a member of the deadly nightshade family. Thought by some to be poisonous, it was given the botanical name *Lycopersicon* (wolf peach). Only later was *escuentum*, or *edible*, added to the title. It is good to remember, though, that the leaves and stems of the tomato *are* indeed poisonous. Always one to experiment, Thomas Jefferson grew yellow tomatoes for conserve in 1792, but the discussion about the edibility of tomatoes raged well into the nineteenth century.

Since the tomato develops from the ovary of a flower enclosing the developing seed, it is technically a fruit. But in 1893 the United States Supreme Court decreed otherwise. When a tariff case involving taxes on imported vegetables appeared before the high court, the justices ruled that since the tomato was almost always eaten with or as part of the main course, it was a vegetable in spite of what the botanists and the defendant chose to call it.

Fresh, vine-ripened tomatoes sliced for salads; canned tomatoes, as paste, sauce, and puree; dried tomatoes or preserved in oil—all are a cook's best friend for adding flavor and inexpensive bulk (with few calories) to food. Tomatoes have a reputation as a good source of vitamin C, but even those that are ripened on the vine contain less vitamin C than green peppers and cantaloupe. Being harvested green and subjected to prolonged high cooking temperatures reduces the C content even further. When preparing fresh tomatoes for canning or salads, it's important to remember that the most nutritious part of the vegetable is the gellike coating around the seeds.

In cooking, such diverse herbs as fennel, oregano, basil, tarragon, chili peppers, cumin, cinnamon, and saffron enhance the sweet acid taste of tomatoes. At Sage Cottage we use fresh homegrown tomatoes when we can get them and the canned Italian plum variety when tomatoes are out of season. Drained plum tomatoes have more flavor and nutrition than those expensive picked-too-soon rocks that pass for tomatoes in the produce section in winter.

Tomatoes are a symbol of power, love, protection, and prosperity. When you cut into that first fresh, red, ripe, juicy vine-ripened tomato of the season, you indeed feel as rich as Croesus.

Red Rice Salad

SERVES 6

2 cups water

$\frac{1}{2}$ cup white grape juice

1 cup uncooked brown rice

2 tablespoons tomato paste

$\frac{1}{2}$ cup minced fresh garlic chives (or, if you're doing this in the
winter, use $\frac{1}{4}$ cup minced shallots)

1 teaspoon minced fresh mint (or $\frac{1}{4}$ teaspoon dried)

1 tablespoon minced fresh basil (or 1 teaspoon dried)

$\frac{1}{4}$ cup basil garlic or brown rice vinegar

2 tablespoons olive oil

1 large fresh tomato, diced (or 2 canned plum tomatoes, squeezed
dry and diced)

fresh grapes or cherry tomatoes for garnish

Combine water and grape juice and bring to a boil. Add rice and tomato paste, stir, and reduce heat to low. Cover with a tight-fitting lid and cook without peeking for 40 to 50 minutes. Remove lid; if all of the liquid hasn't been absorbed, allow the rice to cook without the lid for a few minutes longer. Add herbs, vinegar, and oil, stirring lightly to blend. Cover and refrigerate for several hours. Just before serving, add diced tomato and toss lightly. Garnish with fresh grapes or cherry tomatoes.

Fresh Tomato Soup

SERVES 6–8

This is strictly a summer soup to be enjoyed when tomatoes are at their most plentiful.

4 pounds fresh ripe tomatoes, peeled and quartered
1 tablespoon minced fresh sage
1 tablespoon minced fresh thyme
1 teaspoon minced fresh marjoram
1 tablespoon minced fresh savory
1 garlic clove, minced
2 tablespoons minced onion
fresh sage leaves and calendula petals for garnish

Combine all ingredients except the minced onion in a large saucepan. Bring just to a boil and remove from heat. Press the mixture through a food mill. Stir in minced onion. Chill. Garnish with sage leaves and calendula blossoms.

Serve with warm garlic bread.

Tastier Tomatoes for Trickier Climes

Tomatoes are finicky creatures. They need a constant supply of water to prevent splitting. And in order to set fruit, the temperatures must be above 50 degrees. To grow tomatoes successfully in arid areas, the best crops can be produced by setting the plants in a 10-inch hole much the way native New Mexicans planted their corn. The sides of the hole shade the roots of the plant, preventing evaporation of the water and assuring a more even moisture level.

If your spring comes late and your summer ends early, or you have cold nights to contend with, plant tomatoes in a sunny, sheltered location next to a wall that will retain the heat of the sun, ameliorating the rapid drop in the temperature when the sun goes down.

Seedsmen in the Northwest and Northeast have developed more than fifty varieties of tomatoes, some of Siberian descent, that will set fruit down to 38 degrees. These varieties work particularly well where the growing season is short.

Plant people are also breeding tomatoes with a higher vitamin C content. Check your local Cooperative Extension for the varieties that will work best in your locale.

A COUNTY FAIR
August

Herbs for Jams and Jellies

Some experts suggest that fairs origi-
nated in ancient Egypt. There, when
the Nile overflowed, the populace
crowded onto barges to attend festivals
in the cities along the river. In medieval
Europe, fairs and festivals occurred at
fixed times in sacred places; religion as
well as trade and pleasure were the
objectives of these celebrations.

County fairs in the United States
are reminiscent of these earlier gatherings. Though most lack a religious
focus, the American county fair is
also a celebration of plenty, of community, and of pride in the fruits of
labor.

After the work of spading, planting,
watering, weeding, and protecting your
crops from wildlife, both winged and four-
legged, August is the time to show off the
jewels of your garden. Even though we

Queen Anne's Lace
Daucus carota

have become largely a nation of city dwellers, the American county fair is alive and well with blue ribbons for perfectly groomed cattle, tasteful handwork, and particularly, fine jams, jellies, and pickles.

"The rule is, jam tomorrow, and jam yesterday—but never jam today," said the Queen to Alice in the "The Walrus and the Carpenter." At Sage Cottage, every day is "yesterday." Pots of shimmering garnet-colored strawberry, luscious purple grape, and golden apricot jam crowd the pantry shelves and appear each morning at the breakfast table to top piping-hot biscuits or crispy herb toast. All are laced with a hint of the herb best suited to enhance the fresh fruit flavor of the jam. Thyme, rose geranium, sweet cicely, anise, and basil all lend a special touch to the more than 200 half-pints of homemade jams and jellies we make in the Sage Cottage kitchen each year.

Once upon a time, jam making was a long steamy process. Cooking fruit to the proper jellying consistency created a sauna in the kitchen and was an iffy process at best. The more humid the day, the longer the jam cooked—and the hotter the cook became.

In the dim, dark past I was a purist, thinking that the only way to make jam was the old-fashioned way. Then I tried low-sugar jams made with powdered pectins. A new, cooler day dawned. These pectins need one-third less sugar than other pectins and are faster and easier to use as well. Sure-Jell Light and Slim Set are the brand names for pectins that allow you to cut the sugar in your jams and to cook those jams for four minutes rather than forty-five. (Sure-Jell Light is easier to find at the grocer near Sage Cottage, so that's the one I use most often).

Several years ago, an *Organic Gardening* nutritionist experimented with several brands of pectins. She tried everything from the conventional boil-it-down method to products that use no added sugar. The conclusion was that while the jams produced with less sugar were a bit paler in color, they had a decidedly fruitier taste that was preferred by many of the taste testers. Jams with no sugar seemed flat and uninteresting. The low-sugar jams have a third less calories (41 for conventional jams, 26 for Sure-Jell Light), but cost about one-third more per cup of jam than traditional jams.

This summer, try your hand at herb jams. We've offered the recipes for a few of the Sage Cottage favorites. Try these; then create your own jam/herb blends. Experiment: Take a piece of ripe fruit out into the herb garden. Nibble a leaf of herb and then take a taste of the fruit. Before long, you'll find a combination that magically makes the fruit taste better. No herb garden? You can go through exactly the same process with the dried herbs on your kitchen shelf. Dried herbs are more potent, so use less. The taste of the herb should be elusive—a mere hint of added flavor that doesn't dominate the mixture. Combine your discoveries in the jam kettle and you will have created your own personal toast topper.

It is important to very carefully read the "Directions for Cooked Jams" that come with the pectin. The mixture cooks for so little time that it is vital to chop or crush the fruit very fine. Rinse and then dry the herbs and add as directed. Since it is possible that the directions and quantities shown on the pectin packages may change, we have indicated the type of jam recipe on the package that would be closest to the one in our recipe. Do not substitute regular pectin for Sure-Jell Light; if you do, your jam will be runny. For perfect jam, follow the directions on the package scrupulously. Then head for the fair to pick up your blue ribbon.

CAUTION! These recipes are designed for use with Sure-Jell Light only. Do not use regular Sure-Jell, or you will end up with syrup.

Queen Anne's Lace Jelly II

6 CUPS

Janet Holmes served the original of this recipe to an enthusiastic audience at an herb symposium in Ithaca. After it appeared in our quarterly newsletter, "Sage Advice," readers requested a low-sugar version.

 2 cups very firmly packed Queen Anne's Lace flowers cut from
    the stems
 4³/₄ cups boiling water
 3¹/₂ cups granulated sugar (1¹/₂ pounds)
 1 package Sure-Jell Light
 4¹/₂ tablespoons strained lemon juice

Slosh flowers through cold water to remove bugs. Cover with 4³/₄ cups boiling water, cover container, and allow to steep for 15 minutes. Strain.

Measure 4¹/₂ cups of the strained infusion into a large kettle. Mix ¹/₄ cup of the sugar with the Sure-Jell, and stir it into the liquid in the kettle. Bring to a full rolling boil, immediately stir in the remaining sugar, and boil for 1 minute. Remove from the heat. Stir in lemon juice. Skim foam from the top of the jelly with a metal spoon and immediately pour into sterile jars, cover with sterile lids, and seal.

Apricot Rose Geranium Jam

7³/4 CUPS

3¹/2 pounds fresh apricots
1 tablespoon finely minced rose geranium leaves
1 tablespoon lemon juice
4¹/2 cups sugar
1 package Sure-Jell Light
8 whole rose geranium leaves

Pit but do not peel apricots. Chop fine. Measure 6 cups chopped apricots. Put apricots, finely minced rose geranium leaves, and lemon juice into a large kettle. Follow "Directions for Cooked Jam" that come with the pectin.

Dip each whole rose geranium leaf in boiling water, dry on paper towels, and set aside. After you've poured the jam into the sterilized jars, top each jar with a geranium leaf and seal as directed.

This jam is lovely on toasted lemon bread.

Gingery Plum Jam

9 CUPS

4 pounds red plums (not 4$\frac{1}{2}$ pounds as shown in the package
    directions)
orange juice as needed
1 teaspoon grated orange rind
1 tablespoon freshly grated ginger (If you use frozen ginger, allow
    it to thaw somewhat before measuring.)
5$\frac{1}{4}$ cups sugar
1 package Sure-Jell Light

Pit but do not peel the plums. Chop fine. Place chopped plums in a
saucepan, and add $\frac{1}{2}$ cup orange juice. Bring to a boil, cover, and simmer
over low heat for 5 minutes. Measure plums and add more orange juice to
make 7$\frac{1}{4}$ cups. Put into a large kettle. Add orange rind and ginger. Follow "Directions for Cooked Jam" that come with the pectin.

    When mixed into nonfat yogurt, this jam satisfies as a snack or
dessert.

More Jams and Jellies á la Herbs

Herb jam combinations you might want to try:

- 2 tablespoons fresh minced tarragon in blueberry jam or grape jam
- ¼ cup minced fresh sweet cicely for strawberry jam
- 1 tablespoon vanilla added to black raspberry jam
- 1 tablespoon minced fresh mint plus 2 teaspoons grated orange peel in cherry jam
- In the recipe for peach jam, replace 2 cups peaches with 2 cups drained and chopped tomatoes and 1 tablespoon fresh mint

And herb jellies you won't want to miss:

For jellies heat 1 cup of the juice called for in the recipe to boiling, stir in the herbs, cover, and allow to steep for 15 minutes. Strain. Add to remaining juice in the recipe and proceed as directed.

- ¼ teaspoon each dried marjoram, oregano, savory, and thyme with cider or apple juice
- 2 tablespoons cider vinegar plus 2 tablespoons minced fresh sage with unsweetened white grape juice
- 2 tablespoons minced fresh basil with orange juice

SENECA CORN FESTIVAL
Late Summer

Corn

In the region now known as New York state, as summer wound down and the time for the final corn harvest neared, the Senecas of the Irquois confederacy gathered for the Green Corn Festival to honor Earth Mother's daughters, called "Deohako," guardians of corn, bean, and squash.

From the Senecas and other Northeastern Woodland nations to the Mississippi Mound Builders and the Cliff Dwellers of the South-west, corn was the staple crop usu-ally tended by the women. Although Indian corn (*Zea mays*) was called a variety of names by Native Americans, each translated meant "Our Life." "Maíz," according to an ancient Taos corn grinding song, "is the fruit of the gods . . . corn is sacred."

Corn
Zea mays

The history of corn in the North American continent is hotly debated. For our purposes here, it is enough to say that corn is one of the earliest crops cultivated and bred intentionally by humans and that it probably sprang from a grass native to South America. A primitive ancestor of our present-day corn, with cobs just $1\frac{1}{2}$ inches in length, and dating from 5,000 or more years ago, has been unearthed in Central Mexico. Scientific evidence aside, I choose to believe the Navaho legend that while en route to the morning star, a magical turkey dropped an ear of blue corn that grew to feed the people.

The triumvirate of native western hemisphere foods, maíz, pumpkins, and beans, flourished under the advanced agricultural methods of the natives. Early visitors to Virginia were amazed to discover the natives planting three crops of "mayze" each year and garnering crops of grain that out-produced any of those grown in Europe. Boatloads of immigrants were nourished by hoecakes, johnnycakes, puddings, porridges, and breads all made from the amazing corn.

Dorothy Giles in *Singing Valleys, The Story of Corn* wrote: "So corn provided infant America with a backbone while it was developing the use of its legs. America was growing, quite literally, up the cornstalk."

Indian Pudding

SERVES 8

This is a traditional New England dish made a bit lighter for our more sedentary life-style.

2$\frac{1}{2}$ cups hot milk
$\frac{1}{4}$ cup cornmeal
1 teaspoon sugar
$\frac{1}{4}$ teaspoon baking soda
$\frac{1}{3}$ cup maple syrup
1 cup cold milk
$\frac{1}{2}$ cup raisins or currants

Heat milk in the top of a double boiler and slowly stir in cornmeal; continue stirring over boiling water until mixture thickens. Combine sugar and baking soda and stir into cornmeal mixture. Stir in maple syrup and cold milk thoroughly. Add raisins. Pour all into a lightly oiled 1$\frac{1}{2}$-quart casserole. Bake at 275° F for 2 hours. Serve warm topped with yogurt or light ice cream.

———

Corn and Three-Bean Casserole

SERVES 6–8

Corn is deficient in the amino acid lysine, a lack of which can cause both protein and niacin deficiencies and eventually result in pellagra. Beans are high in lysine, so this dish is a nutritional bargain.

1 tablespoon corn or sunflower seed oil

1 large green pepper, chopped

1 large onion, chopped

2 cloves garlic

1 6-ounce can green chilies

2 bay leaves

1 tablespoon minced fresh summer savory (or 1$\frac{1}{2}$ teaspoons dried)

$\frac{1}{2}$ teaspoon ground cumin

3 tablespoons minced fresh bee balm leaves (or 1 rounded
   tablespoon dry)

   or

   1$\frac{1}{2}$ tablespoons minced fresh mint combined with 1$\frac{1}{2}$
      tablespoons minced fresh oregano (or 2 teaspoons each dried)

1 package frozen corn kernels

1 1-pound can pinto beans

1 1-pound can black beans

1 8-ounce can tomato sauce

$\frac{1}{4}$ cup coarsely chopped sunflower seeds

Heat oil over medium heat in a large ovenproof casserole. Add green pepper, onion, and garlic. Cook until onion is transparent. Stir in green chilies and herbs. Add corn and beans, two bean cans of water, and tomato sauce; stir to blend. Bake covered in a 325° F oven for 30 minutes. Remove cover. Sprinkle sunflower seeds over the top. Return to oven and cook for an additional 15 minutes.

Serve with lettuce and sliced tomatoes topped with salsa.

Oven-Baked Corn

Corn on the cob is a uniquely American dish and requires special table rules for its consumption. In 1844, diners were warned by Charles Day in *Hints of Etiquette* that "It is not elegant to gnaw Indian corn. The kernels should be scored with a knife, scraped on the plate, and then eaten with a fork." *Hints on Etiquette* notwithstanding, this corn is meant to be gnawed on with relish and delight.

Pull back the husks of the corn, leaving them attached to the stem. Pull off the silk and brush to remove it all. Rub each ear with a sprig of minced summer savory. Carefully pull the husks back up around the corn. Add 1 tablespoon sugar to a large kettle of water and plunge ears in the water. Soak for 1 hour. Shake off the water. Bake ears on the oven rack at 400° F for 30 minutes. Serve in the husks.

A-maiz-ing Taste

For the best-tasting corn, cooks are advised to put a kettle of water on the stove, add a tablespoon of sugar, wait until the water boils, then race to the garden to pick the corn. The sugar in corn turns to starch after picking, so its sweet flavor is often lost long before you bring it home from the market. If you don't have a cornfield in the backyard, look for fresh-looking green husks with golden brown silk. The silk should be slightly damp and soft. Small, full kernels will be more tender than large ones. Cook and eat corn as quickly as possible after picking or purchasing it.

If storage is necessary, refrigerate the corn in the husk. Husk just before cooking. Avoid overcooking; modern varieties of corn are sweeter and more tender than those in our mothers' day.

SEPTEMBER

In September, the harvest moon (that full moon closest to the autumnal equinox) beams over the land, extending the farmer's working day well into the night. While this phenomenon is more evident in Europe than in the lower latitudes of upstate New York, the full moon of fall still sheds a magic light on the fading garden at Sage Cottage.

This is the time to reflect on the summer past—to celebrate the successes of this year's garden and make plans to avoid failures in the year to come.

It's time to take heart in Jonathan Swift's declaration: "Who ever makes two ears of corn, or two blades of grass to grow, where only one grew before, deserves better of mankind, and does more essential service to his country than the whole race of politicians put together."

LABOR DAY
The First Monday in September

Herbs and Labor-Saving Meals

Labor Day, the first Monday in September, was linked to the mainstream of the late nineteenth-century labor movement. First observed in 1882, it was originally dedicated to the "working class" of the new industrial age. The first Labor Day celebrations seemed to reflect Ulysses S. Grant's idea that "what ever there is of greatness in the United States, or indeed in any other country, is due to labor. The laborer is the author of all greatness and wealth. Without labor there would be no government, and no leading class, and nothing to preserve."

Peter J. McGuire of the Central Labor Union of New York City hoped that the choice of an early September holiday would also prove a boon to the hard-working people in whose honor the day was set aside. Falling between July 4 and Thanksgiving, Labor Day, McGuire reasoned, would "fill a wide gap

Lovage
Levisticum officinale

in the chronology of legal holidays" and allow laborers to celebrate "a most pleasant season."

In the Northeast, Labor Day signifies not only our respect for laborers; it signals even more surely than does the autumnal equinox the undeniable fact that fall has arrived. Vacations are over. It's back to school, back to routines, and back to the real world beyond balmy summer days.

By the Tuesday following the holiday, days seem to shorten with a gathering momentum. Though warm weather may persist and the black frosts hold off for a while, our body clocks tell us that it's time for heartier food. Soup has always been a favorite fall supper in our family.

Yesteryear's stockpot simmering on the back stove has been replaced by the modern Crockpot. Crockpots, or slow cookers, are a perfect way to produce old-fashioned soups. If you're away from home during the day or want to spend a day working in the garden, this energy-saving convenience will have your dinner ready when you get home. Crockpot cookery provides an added bonus—the whole house will smell as if someone has been cooking all day. Surely a comforting feeling to adults and children alike.

Unfortunately, the long period of time required to cook food in this appliance has a tendency to wash out flavors. I increase the herbs called for in a standard recipe by one quarter and add the quarter for the last half-hour of cooking. You can also improve the flavor of many Crockpot meals by adding 2 tablespoons of very finely minced parsley just before serving.

Spicy Chili Minestrone

SERVES 6

Italy meets New Mexico in this spicy soup. Serve with cornbread or toasted corn tortillas.

1 1-pound can fava or other white beans
1 1-pound can chick peas
¾ cup minced onion
2 cloves garlic, minced
½ cup shredded carrots
1 cup diced celery tops (or 3 tablespoons minced lovage leaves)
3 cloves garlic, peeled
1 16-ounce can Italian plum tomatoes
1 large potato, diced
1 tablespoon Worcestershire sauce
1 tablespoon chili powder
6 cups water combined with 1 tablespoon plus 1 teaspoon brewer's yeast extract (or 4 tablespoons brewer's yeast flakes)
1½ cups fresh spinach, large stems removed and sliced in strips
1½ teaspoons dried oregano
1½ teaspoons dried basil
¾ cup any small macaroni
½ cup coarsely chopped Italian parsley

Combine the first twelve ingredients (up to and including the brewer's yeast extract) in the slow cooker or Crockpot. The liquid should completely cover the vegetables; if it doesn't, add more. Cover. Cook on high

1 hour, then on low 8 to 8½ hours. During last half hour of cooking, stir in oregano, basil, spinach, and pasta. Cover. Stir in parsley just before serving. Serve with fresh grated Romano cheese and Italian bread.

———

Yellow Split Pea Soup

SERVES 6

1 pound yellow split peas

6 cups water

1 bay leaf, 6 whole cloves, and 6 whole peppercorns tied in muslin or cheesecloth

½ cup shredded carrots

2 cups diced onions

1 tablespoon brewer's yeast extract (or 3 tablespoons brewer's yeast flakes)

2 teaspoons dried thyme (Add 1 teaspoon when you start the cooking, 1 teaspoon half an hour before serving.)

2 tablespoons minced fresh lovage

1 tablespoon minced fresh summer savory

Cover peas with water and allow to stand overnight. Drain peas and add to cooker. Add herb bundle, carrots, onions, brewer's yeast extract, and 1 teaspoon thyme. Add water to cover. Cover. Cook on low heat 10 to 12 hours. A half-hour before serving, stir in remaining thyme with lovage and savory. Continue cooking. If the soup is very thick, you can thin it with warm skim milk.

Celery without the Fuss

The warm, pungent, slightly bitter taste of lovage (*Levisticum officinale*) adds a boost to soups and stews that its umbelliferous cousins, celery (*Apium graveolens*) and celery seed (the fruit of a related *Apium*), can't match. Maude Grieve, author of the voluminous *A Modern Herbal* (Dover, 1971), suggests that it tastes like a cross between celery and angelica; in fact, the young leaves are often used like angelica. Lovage must be used with restraint, for a little goes a very long way.

In early September, so long as the slugs haven't been at work, lovage is still flourishing. Pick some, rinse the leaves, and dry carefully. Spread the leaves between two paper towels and microwave on high for 1 minute. Continue cooking in 30-second bursts until the lovage is dry. Store in a covered container. The seeds or fruit of the lovage are equally useful and can replace celery seed. Use either whenever you want a celery flavor. Dried lovage adds a nice touch to blends of dried herbs, but again, restraint is the watchword.

Lovage is best propagated from offshoots and enjoys a rich, moist soil.

GRAPE FESTIVAL
September

Grapes in Infinite Variety

September. Grapes . . . luscious purple, frosty green, dusty red . . . hang on the vine under the harvest moon. In Nauvoo, Illinois, preparations are under way for their annual Grape Festival. Timed to coincide with the local grape harvest, this festival attracts huge crowds eager to see the historical pageant.

Grapes, symbol of peace and abundance, were sacred to Dionysus and Bacchus. The Romans painted pictures of grapes on garden walls to ensure fertility, but whether this was done to affect the garden or the homes' residents is not made quite clear. Always considered a restorative, grapes were much esteemed medicinally. Their fruit and juice and the ash from their vines was said to cure everything from excess bleeding to piles.

Grapes
Vitis

When Leif Eriksson arrived in North America in 1006, the grapes he tasted were probably *Vitus lambrusca*, the granddaddy of our Concords and perhaps even Catawbas. Eriksson was so impressed by the bounty of this new land that he promptly christened it "Vinland," land of the vines. These sweet foxy grapes didn't contain, as John Gerard noted in his herbal (1633), the "meane between soure and sweete" that made great wine, but they sustained the Native Americans and later, the settlers from the Old World. Grapes were vitally important to the well-being of the Pilgrims and to the survival of Lewis and Clark on their famed expedition. Now perhaps even more than before, grapes figure significantly in many cuisines throughout the world.

As summer winds down in the Finger Lakes region of upstate New York, grapes in all their succulent variety become the fruit of the moment. Favorite American varieties like Scuppernong, Catawba, and Concord sweeten the early days of fall, as do their hardy, seedless cousins Emeraude, Reliance, and Eistedt, which were developed to bring all the pleasure of older varieties and none of the nuisance of seeds.

Few agricultural products offer their bounty to cooks so openhandedly or in such variety as does the grape. The fruits, seeds, leaves, and young shoots are all edible. We collect the liquid pressed from the fruit to make wine, ambrosial juices, gemlike jellies, and flavorful vinegars. The fruit, blushing pink, soft dusty green, deep bluish black, appears on our tables in jams and in chicken and fish dishes labeled "Veronique."

Raisins, the grape's sweet sisters, are produced in profusion in California. The magic ingredient in breads and sweet rolls, these sweet, iron-filled dried grape treats make the grape available year-round. Currants (the dried variety), less sweet and tender than raisins, come from the Zante grape.

The newest member of the grape family of products to be found on your grocer's shelves is grape seed oil. This viscous, créme de menthe–colored oil, long a staple in parts of France and Switzerland (especially for preparing *Fondue Bourguignonne*), is best used sparingly. To my mind, it has a heavy, oily taste not suitable for salads.

This year, celebrate along with the folks from Nauvoo—plan a grape tasting. Collect as many varieties as you can and arrange the multi-hued bunches on large platters lined with grape leaves. Provide glass plates with grape-leaf liners and scissors for cutting small bunches from the main stems. Supplement your feast with some crusty bread and a little blue cheese. But beware! This is not an outside fall feast. If you are foolish enough to lay out your spread in the sunny glory of a autumn afternoon, yellow jackets will quickly join the party and spoil the fun.

———

Grapey-Tomato Salad
with Blue Cheese Dressing

SERVES 4

This is the perfect salad for early fall when there are still lots of red, juicy tomatoes in the garden and the grapes spill over the counters of every roadside stand.

    8 Napa (Chinese) cabbage leaves, rinsed and dried

    3 large, ripe, red, room-temperature tomatoes, peeled and cut into thick slices

    2 cups halved sweet table grapes

    grape leaves

Cut white center section from the cabbage leaves and put aside. Cut leafy sides into narrow slices. Cut center sections into $\frac{1}{4}$-inch slices on the diagonal. Lay grape leaves on platter, cover with the shredded cabbage, and top with tomato slices sprinkled with halved grapes. Pour dressing over all. Garnish with small bunches of grapes and a Johnny-jump-up or two.

Dressing

1 tablespoon red wine vinegar
3 tablespoons yogurt
2 tablespoons sunflower or corn oil
1 clove garlic
1 tablespoon minced chives
1 tablespoon blue cheese
$\frac{1}{2}$ teaspoon paprika

Combine all ingredients in the bowl of a blender or food processor, whirl.

———

Grape Collage
with Orange-Yogurt Sauce

SERVES 4

Eminently simple, this dessert is pretty and elegant as well. The tangy orange-yogurt sauce can also be used as a dip for bunched grapes.

3 or 4 varieties of table grapes (Choose a variety of colors; you'll
    need enough of each variety to serve one person.)
2 tablespoons frozen orange juice concentrate
$\frac{2}{3}$ cup low-fat or nonfat yogurt
4 rose geranium leaves for garnish

Combine yogurt and orange juice thoroughly; allow to chill in the freezer
while you eat dinner. Wash grapes and divide into four footed sherbet
dishes. When you're ready for dessert, break up the sauce (if it has frozen)
and spoon over grapes. Garnish with a fresh rose geranium leaf.

Grapes for the Table

When buying grapes, you should look for bunches with
the fruit firmly attached to supple green stems. The fruit
should be plump but not soft and have a deep color for
the variety. Grapes can be stored wrapped in a paper
towel (to absorb extra moisture) in a plastic bag in the
refrigerator for at least a week. For table use, they should
be washed just before eating and served just a bit below
room temperature.

JOHNNY APPLESEED'S BIRTHDAY

September 26

Apples

American orchardist and folk hero John Chapman, whom we all know as Johnny Appleseed, was born on September 26, 1775, during the apple harvest in Connecticut. As a young man, Chapman wandered the backroads of Pennsylvania, Ohio, Illinois, and Indiana planting orchards and spreading Swedenborgian doctrine with equal fervor. He traveled over and over the route, tending and nurturing the tiny seedlings he had planted until they were able to survive on their own. Chapman's life spanned sixty-one years, but his trees live on.

Apples
Malus pumilus
var. McIntosh

Maiden's Blush, Gloria Mundi, Salisbury Pippin, Roxbury Russet, Gravenstein, Rhode Island Greening, Esopus, Winesap, Tomkins King, Spitzenburg—the names of the old apples that Chapman planted—bring to mind a treasure trove of flavors. Like fine wines, apples, have infinite varieties of taste and texture.

Nowadays, we take apples for granted, but it wasn't always so. In ancient times apples were treasured. Thought to be the fruit of the gods, they were a symbol of immortality and an emblem of fruitfulness.

No fruit appears in *Bartlett's Familiar Quotations* more often than the apple. From the Bible to nursery rhymes, the apple appears as an offering, a test for chastity, a means of divination, and a love charm. In Welsh legends, kings and heroes were supposed to live on after death in a paradise of apple groves called Avalon. The apple was sacred to Idun, Norse goddess of youth and spring—the reason no doubt, that Scandinavians sought to preserve their youth by feasting on apples.

Apples have been touted as a nerve tonic. *The Herbalist Almanac* suggests "If your nerves are shaky, make good use of apples," and we all know that they'll keep doctors away. In the seventeenth century in Europe, the charming combination of apple pulp, pork fat, and rose water was sold as a skin cream while the juice of sour apples was suggested to remove warts.

No fruit recommends itself more highly to the cook than the apple, for it challenges the adventurous and satisfies the novice. Recipes for apples appear in the cuisines of most temperate countries in the world. The strudel and *La Tarte des Demoiselles Tatin* of the continent became apple pie, flummeries, Bettys, fritters, and fools when transported to U.S. shores. Apple cider also adds its essence to many dishes; it can even replace wine in many recipes.

The list of herbs and spices used to enhance the humble apple is as varied as the countries where the dishes are served. Caraway or perhaps sage with apples spells England; cardamom, Scandinavia; lemon, France. Sweet spices, cinnamon and nutmeg, appear with apples in all cuisines.

Used discreetly, each enhances the apple in a special way and, in turn, apples enhance the flavor of a wide variety of foods.

September is the time to take care of yourself. Settle back with a crisp, juicy apple or a glass of freshly pressed cider, comforted by a plethora of platitudes about keeping the doctor away.

———

Tunapple Salad

SERVES 4

$\frac{1}{2}$ teaspoon Dijon-style mustard

1 teaspoon mayonnaise

1 tablespoon plain, low-fat yogurt

1 tablespoon dry white wine (or 1 teaspoon white rice vinegar
   mixed with 2 teaspoons water)

$\frac{1}{8}$ teaspoon dried tarragon

1 medium sweet apple, coarsely chopped

1 5$\frac{1}{2}$-ounce can solid white water-packed tuna, drained and rinsed
   under cold water and drained again

1 teaspoon minced shallots or green onions

Combine mustard, mayonnaise, yogurt, wine, and tarragon in a small bowl. Stir in chopped apple and mix lightly. Stir in tuna and shallots; cover and refrigerate. This needs to sit at least an hour for the flavors to blend. Serve with crisp green pepper strips and warm sesame bread sticks.

Five Roses Eggless Applesauce Cake

SERVES 8–10

The original version of this spicy applesauce cake appeared in a collection of recipes supplied by Canadian women and printed in 1915 by the Lake of the Woods Milling Company, maker of Five Roses Flour. A careful reading of the book is a reminder that the housewife at the turn of the century confined her cooking to the ingredients at hand. Hens laid eggs best in spring and summer, so this eggless cake was probably a favorite in autumn, when apples were abundant and eggs in short supply. It is a boon for today's cholesterol-conscious eater. This hearty, heavy cake is at its best with strong black coffee, a brimming glass of milk, or cold sweet cider.

$3/4$ cup margarine
$2/3$ cup brown sugar
$1^3/4$ cups white flour
$3/4$ cup whole wheat flour
1 teaspoon ground allspice
1 teaspoon ground cinnamon
grated rind from $1/2$ lemon
2 teaspoons baking soda
$1^1/2$ cups hot unsweetened applesauce
1 cup raisins

Combine softened margarine and sugar; beat together until light. Combine flours and spices. Stir lemon rind and soda into hot applesauce in a medium bowl. (It will whoosh up, doubling in volume.) Add half the applesauce mixture to the sugar/margarine combination with half the flour mixture; beat at medium speed until well mixed. Pour in remaining flour and applesauce mixtures and beat well. Stir in raisins. Grease two $7^3/_8$ x $3^5/_8$ x $2^1/_4$-inch pans. Pour half of batter into each pan and smooth top lightly. Bake at 350° F 35–45 minutes or until a knife inserted into the cake emerges clean. This cake freezes well.

Apple Games

Fall brings with it traditional apple games for children—fun that is innocent but rooted deeply in the myth that the apple is the fruit of love. Bobbing for apples was originally a form of marriage divination. Slips of paper with girls' names were tucked into the apples, and the boys hoped to latch onto the one of their choice.

These blushing orbs of the orchard were the fruit of desire. They belonged to the Celtic and Greek goddesses of love. Cut an apple in half and you'll understand their allusions. Your future on the marriage market could be predicted by the number of seeds in a cut apple: An even number meant that you'd soon be walking down the aisle; an odd number meant that solitary splendor would be your lot a bit longer. Find one cut seed and the marriage was destined to be stormy; find two seeds and widowhood loomed on the horizon.

NATIVE AMERICAN DAY
Fourth Friday in September

Jerusalem Artichokes

It seems strange that we have national celebrations and festivals to honor the immigrant groups who settled in the United States while no day has been designated to honor its earliest peoples, the Native Americans. In 1912, New York was the first state to set aside a time to honor Native Americans and suggested the second Saturday in May for the observance. Other states have been slow to follow this lead; of those who did, the date most often chosen has been the fourth Friday in September.

The original citizens of North America had well-developed agricultural practices, an earth-centered religion, and a respect for growing and living things. The bounty of the land satisfied the culinary, medicinal, and ceremonial

Jerusalem Artichoke
Helianthus tuberosum

needs of the ancient civilization that Columbus came upon in 1492. Resources and land were shared, for the notion of private ownership was foreign to the tribes who roamed this continent.

Native Americans relied on the gifts of the field and forest and chose carefully from among this lavish bounty. Trees (beech, chestnut, and oak); wild grapes, Indian bread root (*Psorlaea esculenta*), camass (*Camassia quamash*), and locust seeds were there for the picking. Lamb's quarters, yucca, maples, wild grapes, persimmons, and Jerusalem artichokes added their bounty to this indigenous wild harvest.

A native of North America, *Helianthus tuberosum* (Jersusalem artichoke) was a staple in the diet of Native Americans and settlers alike, and it still grows in exasperating profusion. More recently dubbed "sunchokes" by Freida Caplan, they have become the cornerstone of "Freida's Finest," the largest purveyors of exotic produce in this country.

The rangy 6- to 10-foot plant is crowned by small golden blossoms from September until frost. Resembling a graceful sunflower, these blossoms last well when cut. Arranged in a huge copper bowl with masses of purple asters and silvery artemisia, they complete a stunning fall bouquet.

Whether they were introduced to France by Champlain or Lescarbot in the early 1600s matters less than their instant popularity. Called "earth pears" or "Canadian artichokes," they quickly found their way to Italy. There they were dubbed "*girasole*" from the Latin *girare* ("to turn") and *sol* ("sun"), a name later corrupted to "Jerusalem."

Crunchy, nutty, sweet, and smoky all describe the elusive taste of the sunchoke—flavors only distantly reminiscent of the real artichoke. Rich in phosphorus and calcium and surprisingly high in protein, they also contain vitamin A, thiamine, and riboflavin. Their carbohydrate content is in the form of inulin, an acceptable starch for the diabetic diet. Jerusalem artichokes are a calorie bargain: One-half cup of the freshly dug tubers contains a mere 7 calories (stored, the calorie count goes up to 75).

Raw chokes are a wonderful addition to salad. To prevent discoloration, it's a good idea to cut them up and add them just before tossing with dressing. For this reason, too, it's important to use stainless steel utensils for cutting and cooking. Lemon juice added to the cooking water will keep them white. Many recipes call for peeling the choke, but since most of the flavor is in the skin, this seems both foolish and a waste of time. Instead, scrub them carefully with a stiff brush. Jerusalem artichokes can replace water chestnuts in your favorite Chinese recipe, and they make lovely pickles.

———

Glazed Sunchokes

SERVES 6

The inspiration for this recipe is a wonderful roast potato recipe served at the Venetian Restaurant in Torrington, Connecticut. Lauris nobilis—bay, that evergreen tree sacred to Apollo and symbol of achievement—lends an air of royalty to this simple dish.

2 tablespoons olive oil
3 large cloves garlic
2 bay leaves, broken in half
3 cups Jerusalem artichokes, scrubbed and cut in $1/2$-inch slices
black pepper

Add olive oil, garlic, and bay to a 9-inch-square casserole or pan. Toss chokes in pan to coat with oil. Add enough water to cover bottom of pan to about $1/4$ inch and grind black pepper over all.

Cover and cook 15 minutes in a 350° F oven. Remove cover and toss chokes lightly. Continue cooking another 15 or 20 minutes, tossing every 5 minutes to be certain that all the pieces are slightly crispy and not sticking to the bottom of the pan. Serve as a hot vegetable in place of potatoes or as a nibble.

———

Quick Fall Salad

SERVES 6

$1/4$ cup strawberry vinegar
3 tablespoons corn oil
$1^{1}/_{2}$ teaspoons Dijon-style mustard
$1/2$ cup sliced seedless red grapes
3 tablespoons minced chives
$1/2$ cup thinly sliced sorrel
$1/3$ cup thinly sliced Jerusalem artichokes
3 cups bite-sized romaine lettuce pieces
garlic chive blossoms or Chinese chrysanthemums for garnish

Beat vinegar, oil, and mustard to combine. Add remaining ingredients to a medium bowl, cutting chokes over the greens just before adding the dressing. Toss lightly and garnish with garlic chive blossoms or Chinese chrysanthemums. Serve with corn soup or scalloped corn.

The Choke Garden

Growing your own Jerusalem artichokes is easy—so easy that it's dangerous, since they spread like wildfire. Each tiny eye left in the ground after harvest will produce a new plant. Choose your spot carefully. Tucked away in a sunny back corner with rich soil, sunchokes will soon produce both a hedge and a food factory in one fell swoop.

The roots are best harvested after a hard frost, but if covered with straw to prevent the ground from freezing, they can be collected all winter. Tubers are attached to the plant by a fibrous cord and lie 8 to 10 inches from the main stem. They should be scrubbed clean and allowed to dry, then stored in plastic bags in the refrigerator where they will keep for several months.

OCTOBER

Scarlet, gold, amber, and orange leaves cloak the trees and set the hills on fire. Henry Amiel, a Swiss philosopher, described October as a time when "One feels the hours gently slipping by and time, instead of flying, seems to hover." There are golden days and frosty nights. The scent of wood smoke swirls through the night air and families gather around the hearth. This is the time when, as an old calendar avers, "home becomes homely."

The gardens are quiet. Tomatoes and basil are limp and brown, but parsley is still there for the picking as are the sage and thyme. Wands of lavender anise hyssop weave in the autumn breeze against a backdrop of seemingly indestructible calendulas. At the edge of the garden, tall spires of giant burnet, like pale green pipe cleaners, are constantly bowing to each other and to the dark-green oregano below. And at the edge of the October garden, the purple faces of stalwart Johnny-jump-ups still stand, cheerfully ready to greet the gardener.

LEYDEN DAY
October 3

Herbs in One-Pot Meals

Imagine, a holiday that hon-
ors a stew! In the Nether-
lands, "*Leidens Ontzet*," or
Leyden Day, celebrates the lift-
ing of the siege of the city by
the Spaniards in 1574. Less
than half a century later, Leyden played host to the Pilgrims as they prepared to set sail
for the new world. William
Bradford, eventual governor
of the Plymouth colony in Massachusetts, wrote that Leyden was "a
fair & bewtifull citie, and of a sweete situation."
But in October 1574, surrounded by the
Spaniards, with plague, disease, and
hunger rampant, the good Dutch people of this city demanded that their
burgomaster Adrian van der Werff surrender to the enemy. This good man
told them that they could eat his flesh

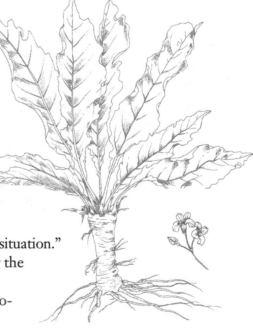

Horseradish
Armoracia rusticana

252

to satisfy their hunger but he would not surrender. Heartened by this display of courage and resolution, the citizens vowed to hold out a little longer. Soon a great storm arose (or as some tell it, William of Orange opened the dikes) and carried the blockading Spanish fleet out to sea. Leyden was saved.

It's said that the first person out of the city that day was a young boy who discovered kettles of a still-warm mixture of meat and vegetables. Soon everyone gathered round to feast on the departed enemy's supper. William's ships were finally able to dock at Leyden, carrying a cargo of herring and white bread. Thereafter, on October 3, Leydeners celebrated the liberation of the city with a lunch of herring and white bread and a dinner of *Hutspot met Klapstuk* ("stew with meat").

You may not have enemy kettles to raid for your dinner, but the next best option is to set a Crockpot going in the morning and celebrate the courage and dedication of the feisty burgomaster of Leyden with a hearty stew.

——

Beef and Beer Stew

SERVES 8

There's no mention in history books about the beverage the Dutch drank with their "Hutspot met Klapstuk," but it's not hard to imagine how good a swig of local beer would have tasted along with a steaming bowl of carrots, potatoes, onions, and beef. Beer also makes a fine stock for beef dishes and combines perfectly with the bread crumbs that are used to thicken this stew.

12 ounces beer
$\frac{1}{4}$ teaspoon ground nutmeg
1 teaspoon caraway seeds, crushed
$\frac{1}{4}$ teaspoon freshly ground pepper
2 cloves garlic, sliced thin
2 cups thinly sliced onions
2 cups julienned carrots
1 cup cubed parsnips ($\frac{1}{2}$-inch pieces)
2 pounds lean chuck beef, cut in 1-inch cubes
4 slices caraway rye bread, made into bread crumbs (very dry)

Combine beer, nutmeg, caraway seeds, and pepper in the bowl of the Crockpot. Add garlic, onions, carrots, parsnips, and beef. Marinate overnight in the refrigerator. Allow to come to room temperature before returning the pot to the heating element. If there isn't enough liquid, add more beer to barely cover. Cook on high for 3 hours and then switch to low for 7 hours. Stir in bread crumbs; continue cooking 1 more hour.

Serve with dumplings or over chunky pieces of cornbread, accompanied by a crisp green salad.

Crocked Pork and Cabbage

SERVES 6

Fall is the time for butchering hogs—a perfect time to enjoy sweet pork. Pigs these days are being bred leaner, so the meat they produce contains less fat than the pork of twenty years ago. Pork and cabbage is the perfect combination to satisfy your family's appetites after a day of raking leaves.

2 tablespoons red wine vinegar

2 tablespoons grated onion

$1/4$ teaspoon molasses

2 pounds pork cut in 1-inch cubes

1 tablespoon oil

2 medium onions, chopped

1 small cabbage, shredded

1 8-ounce can tomato sauce

$1/4$ teaspoon freshly ground pepper

$1/4$ teaspoon freshly grated nutmeg

$1/4$ cup cider

2 tablespoons prepared horseradish

Combine vinegar, grated onion, and molasses. Add pork and allow to marinate while you prepare the rest of the vegetables. Drain pork pieces, reserving marinade. Heat oil in heavy skillet; brown pork lightly. Add pork to Crockpot. Toss onions in pan; sauté lightly. Add onions and cabbage to the Crockpot. Add tomato sauce, pepper, nutmeg, and cider along with the reserved marinade to the skillet. Heat over a low flame, stirring to loosen any of the good brown "stuff" in the pan. Pour liquid over ingredients in the Crockpot. Cover. Cook on low 10–12 hours. Just before serving stir in horseradish. Serve over steamed rice or cooked noodles.

———

Baked Bean Combo

SERVES 6

When I was growing up, my Maine-born-and-bred Grandmother Hallett always baked beans for Saturday night supper. All day long, they simmered in the oven of her coal stove to be served up with hot, brown bread baked in tin cans. Beans are good food and an inexpensive source of protein. Cold, with a little minced onion on thin slices of bread, they make wonderful sandwiches.

1$\frac{1}{2}$ cups navy beans
1$\frac{1}{2}$ cups pinto beans
9 cups water
$\frac{3}{4}$ cup chopped onion
$\frac{1}{4}$ cup molasses
1 cup tomato sauce
$\frac{1}{4}$ teaspoon ground allspice
$\frac{1}{4}$ teaspoon ground cinnamon
$\frac{1}{4}$ teaspoon ground cloves
2 teaspoons dry mustard
1 tablespoon chili powder
1 teaspoon dried summer savory

Sort beans. Add water and soak in a kettle overnight. Cook 8–10 hours on low heat or until beans are almost tender. Drain off water and save.

Return beans to the kettle. Combine 2 cups drained bean water (save the rest for breads, soups, and stews) with remaining ingredients. Add to beans in the kettle. The water level should be an inch above the beans. Cover; cook on low heat 2–3 more hours. Serve with canned brown bread. A salad of crisp red apples rounds out this nourishing dinner. Gingerbread makes a tasty dessert.

Horseradish in the Garden

Pungent horseradish (*Armoracia rusticana*) is not a genteel plant. The docklike leaves spring from a long, deep-growing tap root that is almost impossible to eradicate once this aggressive seasoner has been given a place in your garden. The variegated form is the most agreeable for garden culture. Spreading 3x3 feet, horseradish should be planted in a remote part of the garden. It likes a moist, friable soil. One-year-old roots are the most flavorful and are best harvested after the weather cools in the fall. Take one or two roots, slice in half lengthwise, and replant immediately to assure the next season's crop. *Warning:* If you decide to make your own horseradish sauce by grinding it in the blender, lean away from the container when you remove the lid. One whiff can knock you for a loop!

COLUMBUS DAY
October

Oregano

Columbus was the Wrong Way Corrigan of his day. His voyage to find a passage to the East Indies and the rich store of spices there took him instead to the West Indies, a spot that no one else in Southern Europe knew existed. Other explorers followed, and behind them came colonists from Northern Europe. It wasn't until after the Civil War that the second wave of immigration saw any substantial number of immigrants from Columbus's Italy. Surely they arrived with the ingredients to produce the food of their homeland, redolent of garlic, oregano, and basil, herbs not native to American gardens. Yet even after the influx of Italian immigrants, the use of these feisty Mediterranean herbs was limited. It wasn't until the end of World War II that sales of oregano soared at least 6,000 percent. Soldiers newly arrived home from Italy had developed a taste for spicy pizza, that fragrant pie of tomatoes topped with oregano, basil, and cheese.
The oregano revolution was on.

Oregano
Origanum vulgare

Much confusion exists between oregano and marjoram. Until very recently, in fact, oregano was called wild marjoram. Marjoram, once called *Origanum marjorana*, is now known as *Marjorana hortensis*. In *Herbal Bounty*, Steven Foster asserts that oregano "more properly refers to a flavor rather than a particular plant." In catalogs, we find *Oregano heracleotium* (*hirtum*), *O. vulgare*, and *O. onites*, all touted as culinary oreganos. In nurseries, we can buy *Lippia graveolens* sold as Mexican oregano or *Coelus amboinicus*, sold as Cuban oregano; any number of monardas (*Monarda fistulosa* var. *menthifolia*, *M. austromantano*, *M. punctada*) fill the oregano bill in New Mexico. Even if you discover that one of these "oreganos" pleases your taste, your search for a plant to tuck in your own garden may be doomed to failure. It appears that one of the most important elements for developing good oregano flavor is hot, dry weather. The same plant tucked in a shadier, cool spot loses some flavor. My search for the perfect culinary oregano to grow at Sage Cottage has been about as futile as Columbus's search for a route to the East Indies. The most perfectly fragrant and flavorful fresh oregano in our garden loses its lovely complex taste the moment it is heated.

Oregano is most often paired with basil—indeed a marriage on which the gods smile. Oregano with parsley or marjoram is an equally winning combination, as is oregano with garlic. Oregano *needs* garlic. All these combinations enhance tomato, beef, or cheese dishes, as well as eggplant and zucchini. Used with a gentle touch, they are fine with fish and shellfish. Oregano is as at home in Greek souvlaki as in Mexican salsas, and it is a regular ingredient in commercial chili powders. It appears as often in the sturdy country cooking of Provence as in Southern Italian dishes.

Turkey Kabobs Oregano

SERVES 8–10

Try oregano and tomatoes in a new mode. Sometimes kabobs are a nuisance to do, but with this recipe you can marinate all the meat, use what you want of it and freeze the rest in a container with the marinade. To reuse, defrost in the refrigerator; then drain, pat dry, and broil.

1 turkey breast, boned and cut into $^3/_4$-inch cubes
1 medium onion, grated
$^1/_4$ cup lemon juice
2 tablespoons red wine vinegar
$^1/_4$ teaspoon black pepper
2 teaspoons dried oregano
2 tablespoons corn or canola oil
cherry tomatoes (5 for each serving)
mushrooms (5 for each serving)

Prepare turkey. Combine onion, lemon juice, vinegar, pepper, oregano, and oil; stir briskly. Add turkey and refrigerate overnight. Drain marinade from turkey and reserve.

For each serving, alternate turkey cubes, tomatoes, and mushrooms on a skewer (starting and ending with turkey). Plan on two skewers per person. Brush with reserved marinade. Broil over charcoal or in the oven, turning frequently to prevent burning. Cook 10 to 15 minutes or until turkey is no longer translucent.

Serve with toasted pita bread or in whole wheat rolls. They are perfect for the last picnic of the year with fennel-touched scalloped potatoes (page 199) and a mug of Tomato-Tarragon Soup (page 188).

Vegetables Oregano

SERVES 8

Mild vegetables are made more interesting with a hint of oregano. This recipe is equally good with carrots, zucchini, or green beans, or with a combination of all three.

2 pounds carrots, sliced into $1/2$-inch rounds
> *or*
> 2 pounds small zucchini, cut in $1/4$-inch slices
> *or*
> 2 pounds frozen, French cut green beans, defrosted enough to
>   break apart

2 teaspoons olive oil
3 cloves garlic, cut in very thin slices
$1/3$ cup rice wine vinegar
$1/2$ teaspoon sugar
1 teaspoon dried oregano
Tabasco sauce

Drop carrots into boiling water; cook 6 minutes. Drain. Neither of the other vegetables need this precooking.

Add oil to nonstick skillet. Add garlic and sauté lightly. Add carrots (or zucchini or beans); stir to coat with oil and garlic. Add remaining ingredients and cover. Continue cooking over low flame until liquid is evaporated. Stir in 2 drops of Tabasco sauce and serve. They are very good with grilled chicken breast or pork chops sprinkled with rosemary.

Tomato-Oregano Cocktail

One old herbal suggests that oregano be given to those who are "given to over-much sighing." If you know one of *those* or want a good drink to keep on hand, try this.

Add two 4-inch sprigs oregano, 1 whole clove garlic (lightly crushed), one 4-inch sprig each summer savory and basil to a 32-ounce bottle of tomato juice. Allow to steep in the refrigerator for several days. For each serving, whirl $\frac{1}{2}$ cup strained juice, $\frac{1}{2}$ cup buttermilk, a dash of Tabasco sauce, and 2 ice cubes in a blender. Serve immediately in goblets garnished with a parsley sprig.

The Elusive Oregano

Added to oregano's temperamental nature is its inability to come true from seed, so it's best to start your plants from cuttings, give them plenty of sun, good drainage and a slightly alkaline soil. Then sit back and pray.

To preserve oregano's robust flavor, you can hang the stems to dry or make a strong vinegar from the stems and leaves. Since it's difficult to imagine any dish calling for oregano that wouldn't profit from a little garlic, I usually add a clove or two to each pint of oregano vinegar. Recent studies have suggested that the best time to pick oregano, unlike most herbs, is after flowering.

A NIGHT AT THE MOVIES
October

Herbs in Snacks

In October of 1889, Thomas Edison, in his New Jersey laboratory, demonstrated the Kinetoscope, the granddaddy of all motion picture mechanisms. The history of film was off to a faltering, flickering start. Twenty-five years later, the Wharton brothers arrived in Ithaca, New York, to start producing movies. Neither Edison nor the Whartons could possibly have envisioned the multimillion-dollar snack industry that would spring up as an adjunct to the "movies." After another twenty-five years, when I was a Saturday-afternoon Flash Gordon fan, nickel boxes of Good and Plenty, Black Crows, JujuBes (named after the Chinese date *Zizyphus agrestis*), and Raisinets were about all the theater refreshment stand had to offer. For folks who wanted more for the

**Mustard, Coriander,
and Cumin**

money, Jaffe's candy store across the street from the Lafayette Theatre offered a better buy on penny candy.

Since those innocent days, the proliferation of foods for the moviegoer has been astounding. Popcorn, pizza, drinks in drenching variety, and yesteryear's candy plus more are now sold at prices nearly as shocking as the price of the movie tickets themselves.

The advent of television and the development of the VCR have encouraged the evolution of film into a home entertainment. Americans are turning from the theater refreshment stand to the grocery shelves and home refrigerator to satisfy their viewing hunger. We have become, in spite of the exercise craze, a nation of overweight couch potatoes. Pretzels, potato chips, cookies, beer, soda pop, microwave popcorn dripping with ersatz butter, and frozen pizza assault our arteries as well as our sense of taste. But home viewing has its advantages when it comes to edibles. You can create your own snacks that are less fatty, less salty, and less sugary.

Indian Snack Mix

7 CUPS

This recipe first appeared in the Ithaca Journal under the name Chivda. *Over the years, we've modified it to be less fatty and salty. The unusual, spicy taste will surprise you. Great as a snack and useful as a topping on cream soups.*

> ¼ cup corn or canola oil
> 1 tablespoon mustard seeds
> 1 tablespoon coriander seeds, lightly crushed
> 1 teaspoon cumin seeds, lightly crushed
> 1 cup raw, unsalted peanuts
> 6 cups spoon-size shredded wheat
> ½ cup dried bananas
> ¼ teaspoon ground cumin
> ¼ teaspoon ground coriander
> ½ teaspoon ground ginger

Heat 2 tablespoons of oil in a heavy skillet over medium heat; add mustard seeds, coriander seeds, and cumin seeds. Cook over low-medium heat until seeds start to pop and turn light brown. Remove from heat and put aside. Place peanuts in a flat roasting pan and toss with remaining oil. Bake in a 300° F oven 20 minutes, stirring every 10 minutes. Add shredded wheat, bananas, toasted seeds with their oil, and ground cumin, coriander, and ginger. Continue to cook at 300° F for 30–40 minutes more, tossing every 10 minutes. Cool and store in covered tins.

Oven-Fried Zucchini Spears *(and others)*

4–6 CUPS

Oven-Fried Zucchini Spears make great appetizers during the summer when you've got lots of that prolific summer vegetable. In the fall, substitute sliced Jerusalem artichokes or small green tomatoes (also sliced) for the zucchini. It's also good made with small eggplant slices. If you use eggplant, slice it and soak in cold water to cover for 30 minutes; then drain and pat dry.

> 2 medium zucchini or summer squash or Jerusalem artichokes
> 3 tablespoons dried bread crumbs
> 1 tablespoon grated Parmesan cheese
> 1 teaspoon dried oregano
> $1/2$ teaspoon dried basil
> $1/4$ teaspoon garlic powder
> 1 teaspoon dried summer savory
> $1/8$ teaspoon pepper
> 2 teaspoons corn oil
> 2 tablespoons water

Preheat oven to 475° F. Wipe a nonstick pan lightly with cooking oil. Cut zucchini into eighths lengthwise, then into thirds crosswise. Combine crumbs, Parmesan, and spices on waxed paper. Combine oil and water; toss with zucchini spears. Roll zucchini in crumb mixture. Arrange in single layer on lightly greased pan. Bake uncovered in preheated oven for 7 minutes or until spears are lightly browned.

Barley Sticks

24 STICKS

Sometimes only something sweet will do for a snack. Try these if someone in your family can't handle wheat flour. The sweet taste is from the apple juice and raisins.

2 cups barley flour
$1/4$ cup raisins, whirled in the blender
3 tablespoons canola oil
$3/4$ cup undiluted frozen apple juice concentrate
$1/4$ cup chopped sunflower seeds

Combine all ingredients. Roll out $1/2$-inch thick and cut in $3/4$x 3-inch slices. Bake at 350° F for 25 minutes.

———

Popcorn Variations

The quickest snack to fix is your own popcorn sans butter. The hot-air poppers give good results and don't leave you with a greasy pan to clean. Toss the popped corn with 2 teaspoons of hot oil and sprinkle it with a store-bought or homemade herb mix. Herbes de Provence (page 108), crumbled finely over lightly oiled popcorn, impart a sophisticated taste. If you prefer a taste with more oomph, combine $1/2$ teaspoon chili powder, $1/4$ teaspoon garlic powder, $3/4$ teaspoon dried oregano, and $1/4$ teaspoon dried basil, and sprinkle over your popcorn.

Beverages for the Home Bijou

Movie viewing is thirsty work. While water is a fine, healthful thirst quencher, it is *boring*. Bottled soft drinks have flavor but consume an inordinate amount of the average shopper's grocery dollar without providing any nourishment. Next time you shop, pass up the colas. Instead, pick up some seltzer, that low-sodium cousin of club soda, and head for the frozen juice section. Dole sells exotic combinations of frozen juices with no added sugar. No need to defrost the concentrate before using—just dip it out with a sturdy spoon, put the cover back on, and return to the freezer.

For an elegant sipper, add 1 rounded tablespoonful of your favorite frozen concentrate to a large tumbler, toss in 3 or 4 ice cubes, and fill with seltzer. For a fruit frappé, add 2 tablespoons juice concentrate, ½ cup water, and 4 ice cubes to the blender; whirl until you have a lovely slush.

Add a sprig of mint to pineapple juice. The pineapple, passion fruit, and banana perk up with a sprinkle of cinnamon; the guava-pineapple combination is lovely all by itself, but a big, juicy strawberry lends a nice touch.

Combine half seltzer and half unsweetened grapefruit juice for a low-cal thirst quencher. A sprig of mint is good here, too; in the summertime, it can be elegant and tasty with a bee balm blossom or two.

CELEBRATING THE
YEAR-ROUND GARDEN
October

Sage

Sage maketh the lamp of life, so long as nature lets it burn, burn brightly.

So reads the sampler in our front hall. Sage offers a reason to celebrate in every season. Even after a heavy frost, it holds its own—a few blossoms and gray foliage braving the cold and melding pleasantly with the falling leaves. In the winter snow, its silver-gray elegance furnishes the winter garden, and in the spring, just when you're about to give up hope, new growth appears. Come June, it bursts into clouds of fragrant lavender flowers, attracting every bee in the neighborhood.

This paragon of herbdom, whose name is derived from the Latin *salvare*, "to save" or "to heal," has always been revered. With its soft green, pebbly leaves and purple shaded flowers, common garden sage, *Salvia officinalis*, is the cornerstone of the herb garden.

Sage
Salvia officinalis

Sage was honored by the Chinese as a symbol of immortality, and they traded three pounds of their choicest tea for one pound of sage. John Gerard in his herbal (1633) maintained that "it is singularly good for the head and brain, it quickeneth the senses of memory, strengeneth the sinews, restoreth health to those that have palsy and taketh away shakey trembling of the members." And no turkey stuffing worth its salt (or lack of salt) is complete without sage.

There are reported to be 750 species of this mint family member, the majority being ornamental rather than culinary. A sub-shrub (a somewhat shrubby perennial with stems that are woody only at the base), sage flourishes in dry or stony locations. Fifteen varieties of *Salvia* thrive along the wide front walk to Sage Cottage. Vigorous pruning in the very early spring assures clouds of luscious purple flowers and full, leafy growth.

A low, spreading, dwarf sage surrounded by nasturtiums, self-seeded calendulas, scarlet pimpernel (*Anagallis arvensis*), and love-in-a-mist (*Nigella damascena*) anchors one corner of the Sage Cottage Kitchen Garden and is a delight to the eye. In the fall, we trim the top 3 or 4 inches of the dwarf sage and dry it; it is then wired to a small wire ring to create a quick and useful kitchen wreath. Bunches of the seed heads add a decorative touch.

We pick our sage all winter long but also dry some for use when the garden is blanketed with snow. The drying needs to be done carefully as the heavy leaves and thick stems can retain moisture, creating a musty taste when stored in a covered container. As with most herbs, store in the largest bits possible. Belsinger and Dille, in the wonderfully imaginative *Cooking with Herbs* (Van Nostrand, 1984), suggest that grinding the leaves destroys the lemony taste, leaving only the harsher camphor flavor. You can avoid this possibility by purchasing only rubbed sage in the store.

Sage, along with thyme, savory, and marjoram is the prime ingredient in poultry seasoning, but sage may not be as old a tradition with the Thanksgiving bird as we may think. "Amelia Simmons, Orphan," in her 1796 book *American Cookery*, wrote "Sage is used in Cheese and Pork, but not generally approved." Nearly two centuries later, Minnie Muenscher in her cookbook tells of using it in stuffings and corn bread; sometimes she even tucked a sage leaf under sugar cookies.

Sage was thought to be a digestive, so it's little wonder that it appears with fatty dishes like pork, liver, and sausage. It marries well with eggs and cheese and is lovely with apples.

Keeping in mind that the old saying "Why should a man die whilst Sage grows in his garden?" applies equally to women, tend your sage plants with all the TLC you can muster.

Cornmeal Sage Biscuits

THIRTY 1½-INCH BISCUITS
FOURTEEN 2-INCH BISCUITS

1¼ cups white flour
¾ cup yellow cornmeal
2 teaspoons baking powder
¼ teaspoon baking soda
⅛ teaspoon freshly ground pepper
1¾ teaspoons minced fresh sage, or ¾ teaspoon crumbled dry sage
4 tablespoons margarine or vegetable oil
⅔ to ¾ cup apple juice
1 egg white, lightly beaten
14 small, fresh sage leaves or 30 very small ones

Combine first 6 ingredients in a medium bowl; cut in margarine with pastry blender or two knives until pieces are the size of peas. With a fork, lightly stir in ⅔ cup of juice until dough is moistened and pulls away from sides of bowl. If it seems too dry, add a bit more apple juice. Dump dough onto lightly floured board and roll lightly to ¾-inch thickness. Fold in thirds, roll lightly, and fold in thirds again. Roll out to ½-inch thickness. Cut into rounds with 1½-inch or 2-inch cookie cutter. Gather cuttings, reroll lightly, and cut more biscuits. Place biscuits, touching, on a cookie sheet. Dip each sage leaf lightly in the egg white and place one on top of each biscuit. Bake at 425° F 12 minutes or until lightly browned.

Serve with chutney or a wild grape jelly or filled with tiny, thinly sliced pieces of turkey or with turkey salad.

Peppery Sage Cheese

ONE 8-OUNCE CHEESE

5 cups 2-percent low-fat milk

juice of one lemon

(If you're in a hurry, drain a 1-pound container of low-fat plain
yogurt, with no gelatin added, through a dampened cheesecloth
or coffee filter. Begin directions with second paragraph.)

1/4 teaspoon freshly ground pepper

1/8 teaspoon chili powder

2 teaspoons olive oil

12 large, fresh sage leaves

Bring milk to a boil, stir in lemon juice, and remove from heat. Continue
stirring until curds separate from the whey. Pour through a strainer lined
with a dampened paper towel. Allow to drain at least 2 hours. Squeeze to
remove as much water as possible. (Save the whey for soups, for the liquid
in bread, or to boil rice.)

Add pepper and chili powder and work into cheese mixture until it
is smooth. Form into a ball. Gently spread olive oil over the entire surface
of the cheese. Lightly press sage leaves around the ball from bottom to
top. Garnish with fresh or dried sage blossoms.

Serve with whole wheat crackers.

Resurrecting Sage

But within itself is the germ of civil war;
For unless the new growth is cut away, it turns
Savagely on its parent and chokes to death
The older stems in bitter jealousy.

— *Hortulus*, Walafrid Strabo (809–849)

While I haven't actually seen the ungrateful sage child turn on the parent plant, sage does peter out. Most herb books suggest replacing sage plants after three or four years. This is no chore if you use this method: First remove a few leaves 6 inches from the tip of a long branch; next bend the branch down to the ground, covering the defoliated section with a bit of dirt; then weighing the branch down with a rock. After roots form, you can cut the fledgling from its parent and plant it. If you let sage go to seed, you may get a collection of hardy seedlings. Sage needs full sun and in cold climates appreciates a winter cover of pine branches.

NOVEMBER

Called *Windmonath* ("wind month") by the Anglo-Saxons, November is often rescued from complete disaster by the redeeming warmth of Indian summer. Even though the saffron crocuses continue to bloom, the garden is in its winter mode. Stalks of fennel and tansy dance in the cold wind. The brown pods of the blue flag iris, spent hydrangeas, and false indigo seed heads furnish the early winter garden.

Joseph Wood Krutch noted in *The Twelve Seasons* (Ayer Company, 1949) that by November "Growth is no longer taken for granted. There is a pause and we have got used to standing still. We look forward instead of back, and winter which once seemed inconceivable, now promises pleasures of its own."

The garden year is over.

LOS DÍAS DE LOS MUERTOS
November 2

Chili Peppers

Dancing skeletons, fireworks, parades, tiny coffins from which a skeleton springs with the pull of a string, skulls with tinsel eyes—all are part of *Los Días de los Muertos*, "the Days of the Dead," Mexico's annual mourning celebration. On November 2, the dead are tempted with their favorite foods to return to their families for a little while. This ritual arises from the Aztec tradition that life is more important than dying and life might just as well be fun. It coincides with the Roman Catholic Feast of All Saints (November 1) on which tribute is paid to the departed saints of the church.

Chili Peppers
Capsicum

The following day, on *Los Días de los Muertos*, families gather in the cemeteries to decorate graves with banks of marigolds and calendulas. Each family expects visits from their dead relatives and prepares *ofredas* ("altars") adorned with flowers and the favorite food of the deceased. The food varies according to family circumstances but almost always includes bread baked in a human form, stuffed pork or fowl, sweet oranges, and chilies.

Oh yes—in Mexico there are always chilies. Other than corn, capsicums (peppers) may be one of this hemisphere's most important contributions to the culinary world.

A chili pepper is not really an herb or a spice; instead, capsicums are vegetables that effect a chemical reaction that irritates membranes in the mouth. This irritation induces a flow of saliva and gastric juices which carry the scent and taste of other flavors to the palate. Used sparingly, chilies enhance the flavor of almost any food. In *Spices, Seasonings, and Herbs* (Collier, 1965), Sylvia Windle Humphrey maintains that a drop of Tabasco or other red pepper sauce used in Cajun cooking will improve even a glass of milk, making it taste milkier. This same irritation induces perspiration and subsequent evaporation, which creates a cooling effect, just the ticket for hot, dry climates. If you've had too much chili, sweet fruit or a sweet drink will help put out the fire. It's no coincidence that fiery New Mexican dishes are often accompanied by sopaipillas drizzled with honey. Foaming mugs of good, cold beer are also cooling.

In Native American herbology, chili was added to combinations of herbs as an appetite stimulant, as an aid to circulation, and as a liniment for sprains, bruises, and rheumatism. Today, seeds from McIlhenny's Tabasco sauce are processed and used in Ben-Gay ointment and red-hot candies. Blended with garlic and water in the food processor, hot peppers are thought to be an effective bug repellent for plants.

Ristras, those gleaming strings of red chilies hanging on every porch in Mexico and the Southwest, are not just for show. The pods, pounded to a powder, are the basic ingredient in many dishes. Where hot food is a way of life, chili powder is just that—powdered chilies—not the enhanced version with oregano, garlic, and salt that we easterners are apt to find packaged under that name.

Green chilies are always available in cans (and sometimes frozen) and are fine to use for *chile relleno* and *huevos rancheros* or to perk up a stir fry. Red pepper flakes, added with great discrimination to soups and stews, enrich the flavor. Tabasco, just a drop, perks up ho-hum scrambled eggs.

———

Chili con Carne

SERVES 6

Recipes for chile con carne are as varied and controversial as religion or politics. I like the fillip that green chilies give to this concoction. Sometimes I even add $^{1}/_{2}$ cup raisins for a surprise taste.

2 tablespoons sunflower or other vegetable oil
$1^{1}/_{2}$ pounds lean stew beef, cut in $^{1}/_{2}$-inch cubes
1 large onion, coarsely chopped
4 cloves garlic
2–3 teaspoons chili powder
$^{3}/_{4}$ teaspoon ground cumin
$^{1}/_{2}$ teaspoon dried oregano
$^{1}/_{4}$ teaspoon ground cinnamon
$^{3}/_{4}$ teaspoon dried mint
1 1-pound 12-ounce can plum tomatoes, broken up
1 1-pound can pinto beans
1 1-pound can black beans
1 small can green chilies
shredded lettuce and chopped tomatoes for garnish

Heat oil in a large nonstick kettle; add meat and brown lightly. Stir in chopped onion and garlic; sauté 5–8 minutes. Add herbs and spices, stirring to blend with meat mixtures; cook 3 minutes. Add tomatoes; cover and cook for 15 minutes. Add remaining ingredients and cook until meat is tender (45 to 60 minutes). Add more liquid, if necessary, to keep from sticking.

Serve in large bowls, garnished with shredded lettuce and chopped tomatoes and accompanied by toasted blue corn tortillas.

———

Chili-Cheese-Currant Bits

ABOUT 3 DOZEN

While not a diet food, these Chili-Cheese-Currant appetizers are guaranteed to please. Make them small because they pack a lot of flavor. They store and freeze well and go nicely with everything from fresh cider to margaritas.

1/3 cup flour

1/4 cup margarine (1/2 stick), at room temperature

1/4 pound sharp cheddar cheese, grated, at room temperature

1 teaspoon chili powder (If you can find real ground chilies, use 3/4 teaspoon of that instead.) If you're a hot food freak, add a little more.

4 tablespoons currants

Combine flour, margarine, and cheese; beat until thoroughly mixed. Stir in chili powder and currants. Drop by $\frac{1}{4}$ teaspoonfuls onto ungreased cookie sheet. Bake 8–10 minutes or until lightly browned in a 425° F oven. Remove from pan, cool on a rack, and store in a covered container.

———

Chili Salad

SERVES 6

Hot chili, sweet oranges, and crunchy jicama give this salad a special tang, an ideal accompaniment to Chili con Carne (above).

Salad Greens
1 12–14 ounce package spinach, washed, drained, large stems removed
3 seedless oranges, peeled and sectioned
3 scallions, sliced thinly on the diagonal
1 medium jicama, peeled and cut into julienned strips
1 bell pepper, sliced into thin strips
1 cup cherry tomatoes or 2 tablespoons chopped cilantro for garnish

Dressing
$\frac{1}{4}$ teaspoon minced Szechwan chili peppers
1 tablespoon lemon juice
1 tablespoon light mayonnaise

2 tablespoons canola or sunflower oil
2 tablespoons water
1 clove garlic
¼ teaspoon dried oregano

Arrange spinach on a large serving platter. Place orange sections over that and top with scallions, jicama, and green pepper. Whisk or blend together dressing ingredients and drizzle over the top of the salad. Depending on the season, garnish with cherry tomatoes or cilantro.

Growing and Preparing Chilies

Hot, dry, poor soils produce the hottest peppers. Those grown in the Northeast can never achieve the fiery authority of their more tropical cousins. Fresh chilies are often available in supermarkets. Preparing them is easy, but be careful: Wear plastic gloves and keep your hands away from your eyes. Run the peppers under the broiler, turning until they are evenly blackened, then pop them into a paper bag for 8 to 10 minutes, folding the top over to keep the steam in. The skins will peel off easily. These skinless peppers are nice to use in cooking, since they blend into the dish without leaving stringy remnants.

MARTINMAS

November 11

Wine and Herbs

The lovely, clear, warm fall days that we relish as Indian summer are called Old Man's Summer in Germany. A time when, as Marthe Bockie Flint wrote in *A Garden of Simples* (Scribners, 1900), "with the repose of age there is a gracious renewal of youth." This second childhood of the year, falling as it does in mid-November, close to St. Martin's Day, is known in France as St. Martin's Little Summer.

St. Martin, Bishop of Tours and greatly loved by the people of the Loire and Seine valleys, was laid to rest on November 11 in A.D. 400. By early November, the crops are in, the animals have been butchered, and the new wine is ready for tasting. Thus, Martinmas is the occasion of a second harvest home to celebrate the earth's bounty. As patron saint of vintners, brewers, and beggars, it's no surprise that Martin's day is set aside for sampling the new wine. Many say

Bay Leaves
Laurus nobilis

that this festival replaces the ancient Roman *Vinalia*, a time of much drinking and the bawdiest of orgies. Some folklorists suggest the convivial and popular Martin is simply a church-approved stand-in for the more licentious Bacchus.

Wine is a food that humankind has enjoyed for centuries. Shakespeare advised, "Good wine is a good familiar creature if it is well used." Wine is *very* well used when combined with herbs for cooking. This marriage of vine and field is centuries old. At first, there was little understanding of the scientific side of wine making. Stored wine soured quickly, and herbs were added to "correct" the flavor; put more accurately, herbs were used to mask the taste of spoiled wine. Fruits, berries, and leaves found their way into the fermenting grapes. From grains of paradise to costmary, wormwood to mint, pine needles to eucalyptus—all added their flavors to wines of questionable quality. John Gerard recommended that "two drams of the seed [leek], with a like wight of myrtill berries . . . put into Wine keepe it from souring, and being already soure, amend the same."

Modern vermouth contains the flowers of wormwood as well as other greens, and the secret formula for Chartreuse boasts 120 herbs including angelica and hyssop.

During the Middle Ages, monks in Europe had the time to nurture grapevines and to plant extensive herb gardens. Those gardens produced plants for medicine and the monastery kitchen, as well as flowers for the chapel. It was only another small step to combine the good taste of healing herbs with their wines. It's problematical whether the constituents of the herbs or the alcohol in the wine gave these elixirs their reputation for making people feel better.

From "making the heart Merrie," to guarding against the sting of the scorpion and the biting of mad dogs, to helping women "in travail," herbs and wine were once and still remain an important part of life.

In today's kitchen, we add the wine and the herbs to the food separately. Since alcohol boils at a lower temperature than water does, the alcohol, for the most part, dissipates in cookery, leaving only a flavorful residue that adds savor but not much alcohol to the finished dish. When wine is used in place of stock, that lovely residue adds an elusive potpourri of tastes to soups and stews. Heated with herbs and then cooled, wine improves the taste of uncooked dishes like salads as well. Wine in soups, desserts, breads, and dips lends a new taste to old recipes. For an unexpected taste treat, try using wine to replace part of the liquid in your favorite buttermilk biscuit, pancake, or muffin recipes. With white wine add ½ teaspoon dried tarragon or dill; with red use the same amount of thyme or sage for each cup of flour.

Pungently aromatic bay leaves (*Laurus nobilis*) have been combined with wine for hundreds of years. John Gerard suggests in his herbal (1633) that bay leaves are a prevention "against drunkennesse" and taken in wine, good "against the bitings and stingings of venemous beasts." Once used for hero's wreaths, bay crowns any dish to which it is added with subtle flavor. It rounds out the taste of light foods like mushrooms and fish and contributes a wonderful fragrance to strong-flavored vegetables like cabbage, broccoli, and cauliflower.

For the greatest gustatory pleasure, add the same wine to the pot as you plan to drink with the dish. This is not a ploy by the vintners to get you to buy more wine—it does make a difference.

Seyval Mushroom Soup

SERVES 6

The pungently aromatic taste of bay rounds out the earthy taste of mushrooms in this easy soup. The maple taste from the fenugreek seems to enhance the mushrooms' natural flavor.

$\frac{1}{2}$ teaspoon fenugreek seeds, crushed

10 black peppercorns

6 allspice berries

6 cloves

2 bay leaves

2 cups water

2 teaspoons grated onion

2 cups Seyval wine (or any light, medium-dry, white wine)

2 tablespoons olive oil

1 pound mushrooms, sliced thin

grated rind of $\frac{1}{2}$ lime

minced chives for garnish

Combine first 8 ingredients in a large, heavy, nonstick saucepan. Heat to a boil, reduce heat, cover, and simmer 20 minutes. Strain to remove herbs and spices.

Heat olive oil in the saucepan, then add mushrooms and lime rind. Cook over low heat until most of the moisture has been extracted from the mushrooms. Add strained stock to the mushrooms, scraping to remove any of the residue left on the bottom of the pan. Simmer together for 5 minutes.

Serve in thin china cups garnished with minced chives.

Beefsteak Potatoes

SERVES 6–8

This is a great way to salvage leftover potatoes; it may even be worth one's while to cook up a batch just to make the dish.

2 tablespoons olive oil

2 large cloves garlic

6 large potatoes, cooked, quartered, and sliced

$^1\!/_3$ cup dry red wine

1 teaspoon dried thyme

1 large bay leaf

$1^1\!/_2$ teaspoons dried oregano

$1^1\!/_2$ teaspoons dried basil

$^1\!/_4$ teaspoon freshly ground pepper

1 small can green chilies, diced

2 fresh tomatoes, diced (or $1^1\!/_2$ cups canned Italian plum tomatoes, drained and diced)

Heat oil and garlic in a large, heavy, nonstick skillet over medium-low heat. Cook 3 minutes. Add potatoes; toss lightly to mix. Combine wine and herbs, pour over potato mixture, and toss to mix. Stir in chilies and tomatoes. Cover and cook over medium low heat for 15 minutes, turning mixture once with a pancake turner. Remove cover and cook 15 minutes more. Turn mixture over from the bottom of the pan twice. The potatoes should get crusty and brown. Turn up the heat very slightly if, toward the end of the 15 minutes, the potatoes aren't browning. Remove bay leaf just before serving.

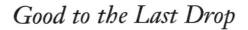

Good to the Last Drop

Use even the tiniest bit of leftover wine to make a last-minute flavor booster. Add a large sprig of tarragon to a little leftover white wine, thyme or basil to red wine; cover and store in the refrigerator. Added by the tea-spoonful, these elixirs will perk up the taste of all manner of dishes without the heavy acid taste sometimes left by herb vinegars. A touch of tarragon wine in tuna salad or sprinkled over broiled fish is heavenly. Basil steeped in wine adds flavor to a single serving of minestrone, while red wine and thyme create lovely flavors in pea soup.

THANKSGIVING

Third Thursday in November

Pumpkins

Nearly four centuries ago, fifty men, twenty women, and thirty-two children stepped ashore on the coast of Massachusetts to begin new lives. After scouting the territory, they decided to settle on the bank of a "very sweete brook" overlooking a nearby harbor. The building of Plimoth Plantation began on Christmas Day, 1620.

Pumpkins
Cucurbita pepo

Stores from England were soon depleted. Corn, stolen from a cache buried by the Pamet Indians for winter food and spring seed, was used to eke out the settlers' meager rations. By spring, stolen corn notwithstanding, half the company was dead. Ill-prepared for life in this rough new land, the whole settlement would have vanished in the manner of Jamestown colony had it not been for the aid and friendship of the Native Americans of the Wampanoag Confederacy.

Planted under the watchful eye of the well-traveled Squanto, the triumverate of Western Hemisphere foods—maize, pumpkins, and beans—flourished under the advanced agricultural methods of the natives and provided the Pilgrims' first harvest.

Pumpkins were called *askutasquash* by the Native Americans along the Eel River in Massachusetts. To the Spanish moving up from Mexico, they were *calabazas*, and at Plimoth Plantation, they were known as "pompion." This "greate fruit" (and its squash cousins), whose cultivation in the Western Hemisphere dates back 9,000 years, found its way into the kettle with venison, corn, beans, and onions to sustain the Pilgrims through their first inhospitable New England winter.

In Plymouth, Massachusetts, on a recent Indian summer afternoon, a descendant of the original Wampanoag tribe was busy stirring a bubbling stew of corn, venison, pumpkin, and beans over a log fire in the Wampanoag Settlement. Nearby in the 1627 Pilgrim village, "re-creators" of the original band of settlers were lunching on a similar fare "boyled all to pieces."

Pumpkin has found its way into cuisines as diverse as Italian and African, yet we think of it primarily for pumpkin pie and jack-o'-lanterns. Although July and August magazines are full of ideas for using summer squash, we have to wait until Thanksgiving before they feature pumpkin. This vitamin A–packed vegetable is too good to be relegated to one appearance a year. Pumpkin's taste is more complex than that of some other winter squashes; it is richer and meatier. Add it to soups, stews, rice, and bulgur or serve it as a solo vegetable, sprinkled with a little fresh thyme.

Shelled pumpkin seeds, often sold as pepitas, are a good food in their own right. In many cultures they are ground and used as meal and have also been a component of religious rites. Enjoy them toasted as a garnish for your pumpkin dishes.

Pumpkin Soup

SERVES 4–6

Begin your Thanksgiving dinner with this flavorful soup, and perhaps you can skip the pumpkin pie for dessert.

> 1 tablespoon corn oil
> 2 tablespoons minced onion
> 2 cups canned or fresh pumpkin puree
> 1 scant teaspoon minced fresh rosemary (or ½ teaspoon dried, crushed)
> 4 cups tomato juice
> ½ teaspoon ground ginger
> 3 teaspoons toasted pumpkin seeds, lightly chopped

Add oil and onion to 2-quart saucepan over medium heat; stir and cook until onion is translucent. Add remaining ingredients and cook over low heat for 15 minutes. Remove from heat, allow to cool slightly, and puree in blender. Return to heat, adding a bit more tomato juice; if the mixture seems too thick, add a little more tomato juice and reheat without boiling. Garnish with toasted pumpkin seeds.

Serve with Cornmeal Sage Biscuits (page 272) or toasted bread with sage butter.

Pumpkin Candy

LOTS!

This recipe is a blending of culinary ideas—more Mexican than New England, this candy is fun for kids to try.

> 1 5-pound cooking pumpkin
> 1 tablespoon baking soda
> 2 cups sugar
> ¼ cup maple syrup
> 1 cup water

Peel pumpkin; remove strings and seeds. Rinse seeds and save to toast. Cut pumpkin into 2x4-inch strips. Stir baking soda into enough water to cover pumpkin, add pumpkin, and let soak overnight. Rinse pumpkin carefully under running water and drop into a pot of boiling water. Cook until tender but not mushy. Drain, freshen in ice water, and drain again. Cut into 1-inch wide strips. Combine sugar and maple syrup with 1 cup water and boil 4 minutes. Add pumpkin and simmer, covered, until syrup is thick and strips are slightly brittle. Remove from syrup; spread on rack to dry. When cool, store in a covered container.

Pumpkin in Other Places

- Use cooked pumpkin in your favorite carrot or applesauce cake recipe (see below).
- Add $\frac{1}{2}$ cup cooked pumpkin and $\frac{1}{4}$ teaspoon allspice for each 2 cups flour to pancakes.
- Chunks of raw pumpkin, peeled, can go into stews along with turnips and rutabagas.

———

Quick Oven-Baked Pumpkin
(Instead of Canned)

YIELD DEPENDS ON SIZE OF PUMPKIN

Fresh-cooked pumpkin has a far better taste than the canned variety and is easy to do in the oven. Remove the stem from a small sugar pumpkin. Cut in half. Lightly oil a pan large enough to hold the pumpkin, cut sides down. Place pumpkin in the pan and bake at 375° F for 30 minutes, or until tender. Allow to cool slightly. Scrape pumpkin away from skin. Use in recipes calling for cooked pumpkin. Pack any leftovers in containers and freeze.

Pumpkin Seeds

Pumpkin seeds are tasty and nutritious. When you discover how much better fresh-cooked pumpkin tastes than canned, you'll fall heir to a mother lode of this seedy treat.

Remove the seeds from the pumpkin. Pull as much of the stringy, orange pulp from them as you can, then rub between two rough towels. Set aside to dry overnight. Place on a large cookie sheet in a 250° F oven for 30 minutes. Remove from oven and spread seeds on a brown paper bag to continue drying.

To toast seeds, place in a heavy, ungreased frying pan. Stir over a medium flame until seeds begin to take on a golden hue. They burn easily, so watch carefully and keep stirring.

I have read that there is a "Naked Seeded" pumpkin that produces shell-less seeds. It takes 110 days to produce it, however, so it is probably best grown in the south.

SAINT CATHERINE'S DAY

November 25

Herbs and the Single Cook

Young, single women once gathered together on the twenty-fifth of November for "Catherning." The object—to enjoy a party, by divination discover the identity of possible suitors, and to pay homage to Saint Catherine, patron saint of spinsters (and milliners).

Saint Catherine of Alexandria must have had her hands full looking after single women, for the life of women living alone in the third century A.D. was not enviable. For hundreds of years, a single woman was relegated to the status of third-class citizenship. Outside occupations were denied her, and she was required to live with her parents, often being assigned the task of spinning wool into yarn, from which we get the word *spinster*. Women without the protection of a family often spent their lives as indentured servants, prey to the whims of their

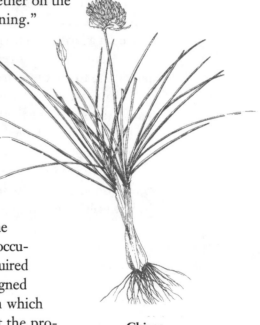

Chives
Allium schoenoprasum

employers. Those single women who succeeded in building a life (often as healers or medicine women) outside the family home were often branded as witches.

Times have changed. Single women live alone, make their own livings, and run their own lives. But no prayer to Saint Catherine has resulted in an easy, pleasant way to enjoy dining alone.

The Roman Lucullus, famed for his lavish banquets, was asked by his cook one morning who would be joining him for dinner that evening. He replied, "Did you not know, then, that to-day Lucullus dines with Lucullus?" Think of enjoying a perfectly ripe pear, a slice of freshly baked bread, and a glass of crystal-clear spring water in solitary splendor and you'll accept M. F. K. Fisher's thesis in *The Art of Eating* (Macmillan, 1954) that one person dining alone on a couch or hillside could reach "gastronomical perfection."

Solitary dining is less daunting than cooking for one. Rather than resorting to frozen foods or fast-food restaurants, take a minute to put a wonderful little meal on your table. In recent years, manufacturers have begun to package many food products in smaller packages. The bulk-food departments offer the chance to purchase minute quantities of all sorts of staples. Remember, couscous and bulgur are the single diner's best friends. Either can be prepared in single portions by simply adding boiling water, covering, and allowing to stand until the water is absorbed. While waiting, you might even have time to treat yourself to a lovely herbal bath.

Cook a meal Lucullus would have enjoyed. Light the candles, find a good book, and settle back to enjoy dining in solitary splendor.

Salad Dressings for One

One of the most depressing aspects of single-person cookery is bottled salad dressing—it lasts for so long! Freshly mixed dressing on salad is one of life's luxuries. Here are a couple of options to improve your salad course.

Mix 1

1 teaspoon mayonnaise
1 teaspoon plain, low-fat yogurt
$\frac{1}{2}$ teaspoon minced shallots (winter) or 2 teaspoons minced chives (summer)
pinch of basil

Combine all ingredients; whisk with a fork. Toss with $1\frac{1}{2}$ cups mixed sliced greens.

Mix 2

1 teaspoon lemon juice
1 teaspoon brown rice vinegar
2 teaspoons apple juice
1 teaspoon water
$\frac{1}{4}$ teaspoon Dijon-style mustard
1 tablespoon olive oil

Whisk all ingredients together. Serve over greens and fruit.

Mushroom Sandwich

SERVES 1

1 tablespoon water
1 cup sliced mushrooms
½ teaspoon dried marjoram
¼ teaspoon dried oregano
1 teaspoon olive oil
1 teaspoon sliced green onion
½ pita bread
1 tablespoon grated Romano cheese
minced fresh parsley

Combine water, mushrooms, marjoram, oregano, olive oil, and onion in a small saucepan. Turn heat to high for 1 minute, cover, and reduce heat to low. Cook until mushrooms are tender. Add more water if necessary. Toast pita and fill with cooked mushroom mixture. Sprinkle with cheese and parsley.

Chicken and Peppers

SERVES 1

1 small chicken breast
1 tablespoon flour
2 teaspoons olive oil
1 small clove garlic, minced

1 red pepper, sliced in thin strips, seeds removed
2 green onions, sliced
pinch of dried basil
1 tablespoon tomato sauce
1 cup cooked couscous

Slice chicken in thin strips and toss with 1 tablespoon flour. Add oil to a nonstick pan over high heat, add meat, then garlic, red pepper strips, and green onions. Sprinkle with basil. Cook until chicken is white. Stir in tomato sauce; heat through.

Serve over couscous.

Deviled Fish

SERVES 1

$1/2$ teaspoon Dijon-style mustard
$1/4$ teaspoon horseradish
1 tablespoon tomato sauce
tiny pinch ground allspice
1 fresh fish fillet

Mix mustard, horseradish, tomato sauce, and allspice. Broil 1 side of the fish fillet; turn. Spread with the mustard mixture and broil until flakey. Watch carefully—tomato sauce has a tendency to burn.

Also check out the meals-for-a-week prepared in one cooking on page 85; simply divide the recipes in half.

The Singular Garden

An herb garden can be miniscule and still produce an abundant crop of fresh herbs. The first summer at Sage Cottage, our kitchen garden consisted of three half wine barrels, yet we had an abundant crop of fresh herbs for breakfasts and our herb programs. This is an ideal type of garden for the busy person living alone, for someone with limited yard space, or for one who has difficulty bending to tend a garden.

We continue to fill and maintain the barrels. One is reserved for tea herbs, and the other two are filled with both annual and perennial culinary herbs, including a few edible flowers.

To assure good drainage, drill several holes on the bottom of the barrel, then cover the bottom with fine screening. Add two layers of styrofoam egg cartons stacked closely together. This helps drainage and cuts down on the amount of soil needed for your "garden." I prefer to use a soil-less mix to which I add half again as much coarse sand as mix. Fill the barrel to within 2 inches of the top.

For the tea barrel, I use one potted rosemary, one spearmint and one peppermint (also in pots), an anise hyssop plant (*Agastache foeniculum*), one Roman chamomile, one mountain mint (*Pycnanthemum pilosum* or *P. tenufolium*), one bee balm (*Monarda fistulosa*) planted in the center with the anise hyssop, and a ginger root right from the produce counter.

The other two barrels are filled with one French tarragon (*Artemisia dracunulus sativa*), one Greek oregano, thymes (two *Thymus vulgaris*, one *T. citriodorus*), one sweet basil (*Ocimum basilicum*) and two spicy globe (*Ocimum basilicum minimum*) basil plants. I also include at least two small chive plants (*Allium schoenoprasum*), and I always find a spot on the edge for a prostrate rosemary and a dwarf sage. Parsley is grown in a large, deep pot separately. Summer savory and calendula seeds are tossed in at random. Everything is watered well and fertilized with a dilute solution of fish emulsion on planting and then every three weeks afterward. Forget what you've heard about herbs thriving without fertilizer; these plants grow so closely together that they need extra food.

INDEX

About the Author

DORRY BAIRD NORRIS is the owner of the Sage Cottage Bed & Breakfast in Trumansburg, New York. The striking Gothic revival house that she renovated in 1983 is landscaped with various herb gardens and brings in hundreds of guests from all over the world, many of whom share Dorry's enthusiasm for growing herbs. In the herb-cooking classes that she offers each summer, participants aid in the creation of healthful recipes using herbs. *The Sage Cottage Herb Garden Cookbook* evolved from the classes. Dorry also publishes *Sage Advice*, a quarterly newsletter of recipes and herb lore.